With a True God Bless

CIVIL WAR LETTERS

Suzanne Meredith

HERITAGE BOOKS
2008

HERITAGE BOOKS

AN IMPRINT OF HERITAGE BOOKS, INC.

Books, CDs, and more—Worldwide

For our listing of thousands of titles see our website
at
www.HeritageBooks.com

Published 2008 by
HERITAGE BOOKS, INC.
Publishing Division
100 Railroad Ave. #104
Westminster, Maryland 21157

Copyright © 2008 Suzanne Meredith

Other books by the author:

Town of Union, New York: Civil War Enrollment and Troop Records

International Standard Book Number: 978-0-7884-4471-5

Acknowledgments

I express my sincere thanks to the following people for their generous assistance in the creation of this volume.

Leon Barrett

Duane & Charlotte Smith

James Phillips

Walter Raymond

Laddie Vana – Old, Odd, and Unique Antiques

John Spencer – Riverow Bookshop, Owego

Ed Aswad – Carriage House Photography

Contents

INTRODUCTION
Suzanne Meredith

One of the most poignant wars ever fought by the United States was the War of the Great Rebellion....The Civil War....dividing people who were previously united in creating a new country.

History is personal, but never more so than in this volume of letters. Love and faith speak from behind the veil of time in the actual words of soldier and kin. In most cases the heart and thoughts of the soldier remained at home. According to the ancient missives a yearning for an end to hostilities was common.

During the four years of conflict 1861 – 1865, letters remained the most important contact between soldiers and those left behind. It is surprising how many letters survived the intervening years. The faded pages provide a very real glimpse into the perceptions and spirit of ordinary people called to perform extraordinary service for their country. Each letter is part of a valuable archive of information recounting a difficult period of American history.

Many Americans became heroes on both sides of the Mason Dixon Line. There were many more who persevered under devastating circumstances...these people never became famous and many died during the war years.

Words from forgotten patriots, both men and women, are herewith recounted...spelling and grammar are just as they were written nearly a century and a half ago. To give an accurate eye witness account of the war, excerpts from official reports and relevant news accounts are included.

The photos and documents used to illustrate the letters were obtained from private collectors, flea markets and some were enfolded in the fragile letters. Many of the pictures were obviously removed from antique books and newspapers so no attribution is possible.

The Broome County, NY Court House is pictured on the day the announcement of the beginning of the Civil War was issued.

WITH A TRUE GOD BLESS
Civil War Letters
Compilation and Commentary
by
Suzanne Meredith

The American Civil War was the result of years of
tension between the Northern and Southern States. Many
factors led to the rebellion including states rights, economic,
patriotic and lifestyle differences...and the issue of slavery.
Abolitionists across the country acted on their beliefs and
formed a system of assistance for those who escaped from
the bonds of subjugation. The "Underground Railroad" was a
path to freedom for thousands of victims of slavery. The
following drawing from an early atlas shows just one of the
many stops on the invisible road.

James Carver owned a large farm on South Water
Street in the 1860's. It was located just outside the city of
Binghamton on what is now called Conklin Avenue. As seen
in the engraving from an 1876 atlas, both the three story
home and barn were large and elaborate. Mr. Carver was
said to be a member of the local "Liberty Men",
abolitionists. He joined Union forces in the Civil War in
1864 and survived to return home. By 1874 his vast
properties were listed for sale, and he soon died from
"softening of the brain".

The site sold several times and was empty for a few
years before being purchased by Dr. S. Andral Kilmer and
turned into a "Cancertorium" in the 1920's.

The barn was irresistible to small boys in the
neighborhood. My uncle Ralph, now over 90 years of age,
was among them. One day while exploring the deserted barn
Ralph ran against a supposedly sound wall and a secret door
opened to reveal a narrow stairway to a windowless room.
Small bundles of work clothes were piled in one corner. A

1

chair and a sturdy trunk were the only other contents…but the trunk was filled with Civil War era letters and notes from J. Carver and family…a forgotten legacy. Many of the missives contained references to helping slaves reach safety. Ralph and his friends carefully replaced the items, removing nothing from a hidden room that was part of the "underground railroad" system.

Res. of the late JAMES CARVER, South Water St. Binghamton N.Y.

Unfortunately no adult knew about the secret room and in 1926 the estate sold to the city of Binghamton for construction of a new school…the old buildings were torn down and buried along with the written memories of freedom.

ORDERS TO FIGHT

As the nation readied for war, reports from officers gave warnings and accolades and predictions for the fight to come. Reports such as these were delivered in every state to give Washington accurate numbers of fighting men available and their preparedness.

Report of the Adjutant General of the State of New York
January 12, 1865 (abstracted from reports)

From: F. A. Conklin – Col. Commanding 84th Regiment N.G.S.N.Y.
July 12, 1864...The railroad communication between NYC and Baltimore having been interrupted by the operations of the enemy, the regiment embarked on board the U.S. Transport Merrimack, lying at the foot of Canal Street. August 10, 1864...Orders to march to the Great Falls of the Potomac. ...Thursday was one of the most oppressive days of the season and the command suffered severely in consequence. Many of the men who had been prostrated by sun-stroke were sent to hospital. Many were removed to their last resting place.
...At Great Falls...while here a spy was captured who was tried by a court-martial and condemned to be hung. He confessed that he held a commission in White's Virginia cavalry. On this person were found the names of all the officers of the 84th regiment, a description of all the picket stations and of the camp...
...An extensive contraband trade in quinine, powder, percussion caps, etc. which had been for a long time carried on by means of the numerous fords of the Potomac was effectively broken up. While here the regiment received the thanks of many citizens for the protection afforded them against the depredations of bands of horse thieves and

3

guerrillas who were supposed to be connected with White's and Mosby's regiments.

From: Wm. H. Hall Brig. Gen.
December 23, 1864 – 3rd Brigade NGSNY
...This regiment met with a very serious loss during the last summer their armory having been totally destroyed by fire which of course destroyed all their arms and equipments.

From: Brigadier General John A. Green, Jr. Commanding Twenty-fourth Brigade National Guard of NYS – Syracuse - November 1864
...I have assumed military charge of the northern frontier of the State of NY...I deem it my duty in this connection to call especial attention to the exposed condition of the frontier and the inadequacy of sufficient force outside of the 24th brigade district and along the frontier for its defense.

From: Brigadier General Henry L. Lansing, Commanding Thirty-First Brigade, National Guards of the State of NY - Buffalo – November 1864
...Owing to the great anxiety of the people along the frontier, growing out of the threatened raids by rebels and vagabonds from Canada the Governor on my request directed me in orders dated August 15, to muster into service of the state for ninety days one company of the 74th regiment of fifty men and keep the on duty at the Arsenal. ...On 19th September a telegraphic dispatch was received here stating that rebel pirates had seized two steamers in Lake Erie near Kelly's Island, with the intention of arming them and preying on the commerce of the Lakes. Much excitement was occasioned in consequence and a meeting of citizens was called at the Board of Trade to take measures to protect the harbor of Buffalo....I offered in behalf of the Commander in Chief to furnish armament and ammunition and artillery men for a steam tug if the citizens would charter one......word having

4

been received shortly of the recovery of one steamer and the sinking of the other with the escape of the rebels to their dear friends in Canada…on Sunday October 30, a dispatch was received by the Mayor of this city from the consular agent at Toronto, Canada stating that one hundred armed men, rebels and rebel sympathizers, had left Toronto for Buffalo or Detroit…prepared with incendiary materials and were determined to destroy everything in their course….For three nights this regiment aided by volunteers from the gallant Tigers, Light Guard and Continentals performed guard duty without a murmur; they knew they would get no pay but felt the necessity of the duty being performed and they cheerfully and willingly braved the rain storm and bitter cold without overcoats or blankets…many gallant fellows have gone forth never to return…the brave men have left a memory behind them that will be evergreen and will add luster to the annals of our State…

From: Major E.W. Lewis, Brigade inspector 16th brigade, National Guard, State of New York
…The northern frontier is comparatively defenseless. Yet we have been fore warned—by the loss of the Chesapeake—by the occasion for Lord Lyons to communicate to Secretary Stanton the intention by refugees in Canada to invade the United States—by the Lake Erie plot to take Johnson's Island—by the burning of steamers on Lake Erie—by the raid on St. Albans.
….the British provinces are filled with thousands of refugees from the south and "skedadlers" from the north all desperate and ready to be set on by the Roebucks of the provinces as well as those "at home" – are sufficient reason to cause companies of militia at every principal place along the frontier to guard the same…

From: Major James Gilbert, Brigade Inspector 17th Brigade National Guard State of New York

…This cruel war still rages and in my view the man who fires on the United States flag forfeits even the right to live under it and ever after has no right to wife, children or property. I trust this war will continue until the last rebel lays down his arms; and sooner than make any dishonorable peace with the vile Jeff. Davis crew, I say fight on till sun, moon and stars go down out of sight evermore.

MISCELLANEOUS WAR LETTERS

In 1861 a young man in medical school in Nashville, Tennessee sent his lady friend a letter discussing secessionist feelings in the state. These thoughts were repeated throughout the southern states.

Nashville, Jan. 10, 1861
Miss Ann,
This is the receipt of your kind missive of last week. Please accept my thanks for it and also for the rapid response. You have my sympathies for the indisposition and hope before now you are restored to the best of good health. I feel glad to mention in the beginning of this letter that I will return to Lexington by the first of February provided I am so fortunate as to get a diploma, if in the instant I fail, I know of no other alternative than to join the Secession Party and embark to Charleston. Don't you think it would be better to go on such an expedition than to return home minus the diploma? There is at the present time much excitement about a dissolution of the Union. The Secessionist Party is gaining numerically every day. I have heard several secessionist speeches, and secession resolutions have passed almost unanimously here. You must not think that I have eschewn medicine and entered the political arena. Dr. Thomas Newton has intimated after his return from home that you and I should correspond through Mrs. Bird. I thought a little strange of it at first but since have come to the conclusion it was only supposition with him, or perhaps some one of our envious friends suggested the idea as it is something new for him to spring a new idea. Please excuse this short letter and all errors as I have written it in haste and I will promise to do better in the future. Respectfully, your friend, Truly, Pat H. Mallory
An answer to this would be very acceptable

Journal entry –
John left home on Tuesday 10 of September 1861 to go to Elmira to enlist. Returned home on Thursday went back to Elmira on Saturday 14. Started for New York on Wednesday 18 September 1861. May God Grant his safe return to his friends.
War is upon us.

Union Col. Elmer Ellsworth was the first Federal commissioned officer to die in the War Between the States, in 1861. As a personal friend of the Lincoln family his death was proclaimed that of a "martyr" to the Union cause....the first Northern martyr in the great War of the Rebellion...although he was not killed in battle, but in a hotel after confiscating a Confederate flag that had been displayed on the building during the occupation of Alexandria, Virginia – the NY 40th Infantry Regiment used the nickname "Ellsworth's Avengers" – his name became a rallying symbol to inspire federal troops to fight the insurrectionists - "Avenge Ellsworth" became a popular war cry.

A War song of 1861

Col. Ellsworth
Entering the traitor's city with his soldiers true,
Leading up the Zouave column, fixed became his view
See, a rebel flag is floating on yon building tall
Spake he, while his dark eye glistens, "Boys, that flag must fall."

Quickly from its proud position that base flag was borne,
Trampled 'neath the feet of freeman circling Ellsworth's form;
See him bear it down the landing past the traitor's door
Hear him groan, "O God, they've shot him!
Ellsworth is no more!"

First to fall, thou youthful martyr, hopeless was thy fate!
Haste me on as thy avengers from thy native state!
Speed me on, through town and city, not for wealth or fame,
But because we love the Union and our Ellsworth's name!

Traitors' hands shall never sunder that for which you allied!
Hear the oath our lips now utter thou our nation's pride
By the hope of you bright heaven, by the land we love
By the God who reigns above us, we'll avenge thy blood!

Zouave – *The original Zouaves were natives of North Africa whose attire was unique, using brilliant colors and garish style. In America the Zouave mode of clothing became fashionable for militia companies who performed for the public. Elmer Ellsworth's Zouaves were known as exceptionally fierce fighters. Turbans, fezzes, and bright decorative clothing distinguished the men from other soldiers and gave them a barbarous, romantic image. Both the Union and Confederate armies had Zouave units.*

Keene, New Hampshire – July 30, 1861

Dear Celissa, Can you overlook my remissness in writing & forgive me for my long delay? Be assured if thinking of you would have written a letter you would have had a goodly number long ere this. For I do not know how many times I have said to myself, "there I must & will write to Celissa. And then something else would come up to take up the time & so it has gone on till I have become a very poor correspondent not only with you but with others for I believe there others whom I have neglected longer than I have you. But I will make no more excuses. Please signify your forgiveness (if you forgive me) by answering this soon. We are now in the midst of haying season so I have plenty to do. I suppose your Father is in the same business, unless he has already finished. It probably gives your mother & yourself a plenty to do. O, I forgot, you have a sister Mary who must be quite a young lady by this time, old enough to help mother a good deal, though she was a little thing when I left Walpole. How do you all do – Johnny & Olive & Father & mother & all. How do you all feel about the sad times? Sad & terrible days have come upon our beloved country, but I believe God will carry us through with a great victory for Freedom & the Right, if we trust in Him. But if we trust in our men, money, the righteousness of our cause or our noble Washington of the present day, Scott, or anything else, & forget to depend on God we shall be humbled by reverses till we do trust in him…at least I think so. He alone can give Victory & cause wars to cease. I am glad to see by today's "Journal", that Rev. Stockton has raised his voice in the pulpit against these Sunday attacks. He says that the ancient Jews lost every battle they fought on the Sabbath. There may be cases when it might be justified to fight on the Sabbath but I think they would generally be very few. We who love our country & believe that God rules among the nations of the earth, can exert a great influence upon the welfare of our country by praying for it & for its rulers. If it be true that "prayer moves the hand that moves the world" & I believe it is true, then the prayers of humble believing Christians will ascend into the ears of the Lord of Sabaoth & they will be answered. Perhaps they may not be answered always as those who pray may hope & expect but we may rest assured that they will be answered in the best manner. How does your Sabbath School prosper and your High School? Is that successful? How is Theron Adams? The last I heard he was quite low & not expected to live long. He is an excellent young man & we all feel very sorry he is to leave us so soon. I saw in today's paper that "Mead" of Massachusetts was among those killed in the late battle. Do you know if it was George or Sumner? "Our band" left Keene today for the seat of War. Write me all the news – anything that you think will interest me. I saw by the Sentinel that a John Marshall was drowned – was he the son of the Mr. Marshall who lives in the Fay & Knowlton District? Yours Truly, M. L. Cooker

This patriotic envelope contained a letter from the war to a friend in Silver Lake...the letter follows....

Frederickburg - June 5th 1862

Friend George, I thought to write a few lines to you to day as I haven't had much time to write since I inlisted. they have marched us like the you know what. we have been out night and day threw rain and mud and haven't seen many rebbles yet. but they say they are in a few miles of us but I don't think that we will see any of them for they keep us guarding railroads and bridges all the time. We have been here about eight days on the railroad. I can't tell where we will go next. We have went about four hundred miles last month but not all the way on foot. We came from Harrisburg on the cars and the rest of the way. I wish you and the rest of the boys was down here. we would have any quantity of fun. I have got an old fiddle down here, we have a dance when we have a mind to. there is a good ball room and pretty girls to. but we don't have much time to dance. I suppose that you have good times in Silver Lake yet. I suppose you folks have got all of your spring work dun. The farmers don't do much down here this spring. I am fraid that some of them will starve before that time. we got six of them (Rebs.) this morning and they look as if they hadent had any food thing for a week. they say that they haven't any thing to fight with but I guess that some of them have got guns at Richmond. Good by for I haven't got any more time to write to day. I am well and hope these few lines will find all of you so. Give my respects to all. From your friend James.

Write soon direct to Washington D.C. Co. K 50th Regt. PV in care of Capt. Mitchell

Brave in the Field—Wise in Council—a true Patriot—Loyal to the Constitution and Union.

Patriotic stationery used in 1862

Lewisville, Va. – Jan. 26, 1862
Brother David, I recd a letter last evening from you & my
wife for whitch I will hasten to answer in my way that is
around one as you well know, my health is & has bin first
rate since I left holm. I was very sorry to hear that your leg
had bin broken. in the first place we have a good supply of
clothes A plenty to eat when the officers don't cheat us out
of it. we are a getting wide awake lately for that our
redgement is attached Hancocks brigade which is composed
of the fifth Wisconsin 49th Pennsylvania G main, 43 regt.
This brigade is attached to Smith's division. we are & have
been for the last three months ten miles north west of
Washington. we are two miles west of the chain Brigade
whitch covers to Patomick. there was an Elmira ridgement
that came here a few days ago and went away whcan I don't
know. if I had of known that Wint was in A ridgement from
almira (*Elmira*) I would of tried to found him. David I hold a
position as commander of a pianneer company. I was
promoted from a second corporal whitch position I have held
since the 12 of Nov. last. You undoubtidly know the duties
of Pianneers is to go in advance of the army when on a
march to clear the way and make & repair bridges while in
camp. I have three teams and one man from each company to
furnish wood for the redgiment. it makes it very easy for me

13

not having any night work to doo sutch as guard & picket duty I thought they had warm weather down south but I don't see it. I never have suffered as much before as I have for the past four weeks it has bin rain snow hail, mud ankle deep. the soil is red clay no stone only now an then a white sand stone. we have new rifles that was taken from the rebels before they wer landed. you probably read about them in the time of it when they wer taken. I will endeavor to tell you a little about camp life. First in the morning is revellee, at seven roll call, Breakfast drill from ½ pst 9 to ½ pst 11, then we all get dinner and ½ pst 1 Brigade drill ½ 4, then Dress perrade then supper, half past 8 taps lights out go to sleep dream of holm & those loved ones. whiskey is cheap only ten shillings a pint, tobacco 75 cts, for lb butter 30 cts. we have a bully set of lads for a bout one weak after pay day whiskey flows, they pay as high as 3 dollars a pint but they must have it. I can tell you David it is a little to steap for me. I bought one pint & got a little owley one day. I made up my mind to hold off for the present. I have a good menny lonsom hours I can tell you but as the old donkey ses it wont doo to put your hand to the plow and look back. I have bin to visit the 86th NY ridgement today but cant hear enny thing of Vint he must be in the **Dickenson guards** down near alixandy. we are now preparing to make an advance. we are to exchange our old things for new improved. new tents, oil cloth, blankets, new coats hats everything for a southern climate. it is now reported that we are a going down to annopiliss to join **Burnsides** expedition. we are to start Tuesday - our things leave tomorrow but where ever I am I will often wright to you & I hope you will doo the same to me. it is of great consolation to me to hear from my folk and old native place - perhaps I never shall return to see you but I hope I shall - I have to good menny dark hours thinking of my family and friends at holm. I have made up my mind that I am stuck for 3 years - things work very slow perhaps for the best - we have one of the boys for a Col. He is a blood thirsty fellow fraid of nothing, young and smart, his name is Vinton - the man by the name of Wm. Movey that came with me from Norwich is a going holm with a discharge on account of ill health - the most of this ridgement are alling - a hundred boys - a tough hard set that will go through thick & thin - I don't know as you can read this - so long I will try to doo better next time.

Owley – *drunk, or pie eyed*

This photo shows the Burnside Expedition, referred to in the previous letter.

DANIEL S. DICKINSON – 1800 to 1866

Daniel S. Dickinson, a resident of Broome County NY, was Lt Gov. of NY State from 1840 to 1845, and a US Senator from 1845 to 1846. In 1861 when the tide of rebellion surged through the land Dickinson traveled throughout the Union using his oratory skills to encourage support for the military. In one of his greatest speeches he proclaimed... "...not one star shall be plucked from the blue field of our insignia or a single thread dishonored..."
*The **Dickinson Guards**, referred to in the previous letter was an independent regiment named in his honor...it was also known as the 89th Volunteers of Broome County, New York.*
His tombstone was inscribed with his words "...The conflict is strong, but the other side is ours" His eulogy read "gone to the maker, pure, the most loyal and incorruptible statesman America has ever known"...photo is Dickinson at the height of his career.

Letter from the War to Newspaper – 1863
Camp Stoneman, Cav. Depot – near Washington, DC
Friend Bennedict – nothing marvelous, exciting or
interesting has transpired in the Camp of the 1ˢᵗ Veterans
since my last writing, and were it not for the continual
prompting of Hib I should let you pass until a more
convenient season. Monotony is king of camp at present and
were it not for the little satisfaction we derive from letters we
should quite "go up" under his reign. I would here impress
upon our friends at home the importance of writing often and
"long". Could you for once be present on the arrival of the
mail-boy and see with what promptness the boys "fall in"
and look at those wishful faces while "any thing for me"
goes the rounds, you would fully concur with my sentiments.
How often have I thought, as I looked upon those sorrowful
faces, when they were informed, "there is nothing to-night
for you", that did our friends at the North appreciate the
worth of a letter in camp their hearts would revolt at the idea
of negligence. We keep steady at the "drill" and I think
considering our advantages we are making rapid progress.
Our horses have not arrived yet, but we expect them every
day then we probably shall "saddle up" and start for the
front. Bully for us! The boys were made to hurrah again tonight over the news from Tennessee. Some have hunted up
the old song, "Old Bumie is the man", and are making the
camp resound with its melodies. How good a little
encouraging news makes us feel. It points to the end of blood
and all such omens are swallowed up with a relish. Grant is
God of the war in the opinion of the 1ˢᵗ Veterans, and any
good thing that takes place within a thousand miles of his
Department is recorded as another of "Grant's bully moves".
As for me I am not particular what Gen. wins so long as he
belongs to our side. What do you think of Mead's last
reconnaissance in force, or rather, his last "On to Richmond"
attempt. 'Tis a general opinion here that he got out of breath
, but as "all signs fail in a drouth", we will wait for the next

train and trust that some good for us may come out of the "old Domiuion" yet. I cannot see the bottom of the movement therefore I will console myself with a Shakespearian idea that "Rebellion lay in his way and he found it". A few days since I visited the camp of the 50th and saw a number of boys from Union and vicinity. I believe they were all "sound on the goose" and generally contented. Pontooning appears to agree with them. Hib says he will write you next week. Please excuse my poor letter for I write at double quick. Hoping to hear from some of my friends in Union and vicinity soon. I am off to bed. Gehile

The 50th *refers to the NY 50th Engineers – letter from Camp Stoneman 1862*
Pontooning – *construction of floating bridges by the army*
Drouth – *the old English word for drought*
(SONG) Old Bumie is the Man - *General Wm. T. Sherman was credited with an effective terror program – Federal Foragers in Sherman's troops were known as Sherman's Bummers – they raided and pillaged on Sherman's march to the sea – the foragers began as Sherman's bodyguard then became foragers and scouts – then transformed again into political avengers grabbing loot, and leaving devastation in their wake. Sherman was said to receive a share of all loot.*
Sound on the goose – *feeling well*
Go Up under his reign – *go crazy under the reign of monotony*
Made to hurrah – *gave a cheer*
Bully – *great – strong term of affirmation*

CAMP OF THE 50TH NEW YORK ENGINEERS

Pontoon Bridges *were a significant engineering tool during the War of the Rebellion. The photo shows the pontoons on the water…*

PONTOON BRIDGE—FROM A WAR-TIME PHOTOGRAPH

NEWS REPORT: War for the Union - Dec. 9, 1863
We have from Washington the news that the two armies in
Virginia are in a state of quiescence, **Meade** on the
Rappahannock and **Lee** on the Rapidan. The pickets are
friendly, and bush-wackers are again plenty. The report of
the removal of Gen. Meade is again revived with a still
stronger degree of positiveness.
The choice as to his successor is said to lie between Gens.
Hooker and Thomas, the President and Secretary Chase
preferring the former and Secretary Stanton undecided
between the two. The army is to be reorganized.

The startling announcement was received here yesterday
afternoon that the steamer **Chesapeake**, which left this port
on Saturday afternoon last for Portland was seized by a gang
of rebel passengers on board, at 1 o'clock on Monday
morning off Cape Cod, the Captain and crew overpowered
and the vessel taken complete possession of by the pirates.
There was some resistance made, the Second Engineer being
shot dead and thrown overboard and the First Engineer and
Mate wounded. The Captain and crew, about twenty in all,
were landed at St. John, N.B. yesterday morning.

Bush-wackers – *Confederates practicing guerrilla warfare*

NEWS REPORT: Dec. 11, 1863
Respecting the capture of the steamer **Chesapeake,** that plot
was conceived by Secessionists who hired some of the vilest
characters of that place to assist in its execution. The design
was to load the vessel with the particular kind of
merchandise of the most value in the Confederacy, and then
run the blockade of Wilmington.

NEWS REPORT – DEC. 1863
The pursuit of the captured steamer **Chesapeake** is being prosecuted earnestly and with fair hope of success. A telegram from Halifax dated yesterday says that the steamer was at St. Mary's short of coal, and if she remained there until to-day our gunboats would take her.

NEWS REPORT: *The Union News* – September 1864
General Joe. **Hooker** is a native of Dayton, Berkshire County, Mass. He married, in California a Mexican lady of great wealth, and on her death, she left all to her husband. So it is pretty certain he does not fight for profit. Gen. Hooker is now at Watertown, NY, in this State, - visiting his sisters, Mrs. O. V. Brainard and Mrs. W. W. Wood.

THE LIFE AND DEATH OF NORWOOD
Journal entry -
Norwood left home on Monday Jany 19 1863 and went to Binghamton. Left home second time August 22 and went to Elmira and started for the seat of war August 26. May God grant his safe return this time as before. Lord we know not the date when God will grant his safe return.

September 18, 1862
Dearest Norwood, Don't know as I'll make out much writing but it is time I was trying in order to have a letter ready when we have an opportunity to send to the office. Aleck brought us a Tribune of the 7th on Monday which seemed like quite late news for us. I went down to Albions but dicided to remain at home until after molasses making. Did you send the other paper of which you spoke to Eldora or Albion we did not get it. Though Mr. Winton very kindly brought us the older mail on Monday. C Redgment 8 Co. E. left on that day

- have had rather dismal weather until today the sun is trying to shine a little. Nellie commenced a two months school on Monday. Stayed with us last night twas the first time. I had Wend milking some for me though I have not been able to do anything since last Friday. I have had to truck about some to keep things (*animals*) from starving. Amanda or I have neither of us done more than we could to help. I think you would not complain of things in too good order now could you look around the house. Concluded this morning I would let cows out again rather than carry them corn today. Besides the yard was soaking wet and seemed unhealthy. The shed has settled so they can not get under shelter for milking or anything else though I did not mind it much so long as I kept well. Sent by milk cart this morning to see if John Levine could go over to Mr. Carstairs and try to get one of the boys to come and stay with us a few days and give me a little chance to take care of myself. I have not dared to take medicine so thoroughly as I ought on account of continued necessary exposure and the weather has been very unfavorable. I do not like to ask Mr. Himan to do anything as I hear so often "they have more than they can do". Hope you are not needing us as badly as we need you. Though I have been imagining you in as bad if not a worse condition than we are this week. Such weather for commencement in camp must be quite trying especially when you were so unwell before. I must confess that I have been almost hoping you would not be accepted – what patriotism you will think! But can not help it. Don't know how many times in my little naps last night I saw you come in – and in dreams the night before – my aching throbbing head was soothed in your arms – not so when I woke though – but enough of this – all is well that ends well and I must look upward where faith and hope will point out bright scenes. Heard from Linda on Monday who arrived safely in Columbus the Friday after you saw her. A nice letter from mother Nora also which will send you. Wolves have not troubled this week as last which has been

one thing favorable. Friday AM – am not quite so blue as
when I wrote the other day. Feel better than I have done for a
week though by no means feel well. Amanda too is quite like
herself again. It looks a little more like getting along.
Pleasant yesterday & today though it was some cloudy this
morning. Have not thought best for Belle to go to school this
week. She & Marie are quite well they want me to tell you
we have had 18 little chicks since you left. Belle wondered if
you will call her darling when you come home. She feels she
has sadly neglected her duty if she forgets to ask God to take
care of Papa. Mr. Webster said someone near Lundersns
wrote home that you were accepted with the others from this
neighborhood. We heard once you had been ordered on to
join the Co. but concluded that could not be else we would
have heard from you something of it. Think there must be a
letter or letters in the office. Amanda is thinking of going
down with Doris tomorrow so we will know. She had not
heard from that school and thought it time she knew about it.
Mr. Geiger offered her a calf to pay her tuition if she could
attend this fall but it has hardly seemed to me I could spare
her so soon after all the rest had gone. Delia was of course
very anxious she should come back there again etc. etc. She
paid me the $4.50 due on her bill. Is it not three or four that
is due him? I have not had an opportunity to send that to Mr.
Benson – thought when Mr. L's people went to Watterloo
would be a good time. Hogs are doing well and nothing else
hurting for want of care as I know of. Wish if you are so
fortunate as to get leave of absence that it could be possible
to have some cement got and a cistern dug – it is so hard to
have to bring water so far. We have been able to save
considerable rain water the past week which I hardly see
how we could have done without – have not tried to wash
either. Mr. Webster's thrashers are finally on hand. Mr. C.
called to get 2 sacks of wheat to take to Mike the other day.
The spike is where you left it – and dose seem but it is likely
to stay. Think this will be sufficient for one envelope so

23

Amanda will write something to put with Mothers. We can not seem to send very often though once a week is not bad if we can do that. Your own Anna. Sabbath Morn – I was disappointed about going to town yesterday. Mr. Garvins people were here in the PM. He is treasurer & paid it.

Cistern – *a reservoir to store water*

The "Tree of Liberty" *was imprinted on this authentic stationery used during the Civil War.*

Baracks – Wed. Oct 22, 1862

Dear Anna since writing you last I had lots of letters as you said they come by the quantity three from you one from Coz Henry & one from Laura today. Also one evangelist. Would think more of the standard clergy. If you got the idea that I was not fit for duty more than half the time you are much mistaken. I have not missed until yesterday since we came into this camp. About the time we came down on the boat we were so irregular that I got a little out of sorts. And Sunday last I set out in the country & et very hearty of the many good things laid before me that I expect I overloaded my stomach. Yesterday I had a severe headache & my bones ached & I had a good del of fever but I took some pain killer to stop the pain & some aloe & rhubarb & feel much better this morn. We drew our dress hat yesterday cost $1.55. We had a draw before for 1 cap 60 cts. Also, 2 shirts, two pair drawers and 2 socks at $4.00. one blouse at $2.25, 1 pants at $3.00 and overcoat $9.50. One dress coat or jacket $5.75. One pair boots $3.30, two blankets $9.20. All told about $35.85 besides saddle. I went over & had my likeness taken in duplicate one of which I forward enclosed to you. The other I will send east. I had on my hat and jacket. My blouse is loose like a sack coat. The picture I sent east has a little more color and I consider it the best. They cost 75 cts. the two. We have plenty of other goods. Everything a man can invent to get our money. I often turn my funds to the advantage of the boys which does me no harm & saves them money. For instance they were paying 15 cts. per pack or 10 cts per dozen for sample you see. I bought 300 for 35 cts per hundred & sold them out in less than ½ an hour for 10 cts. per pack making 40 cts. per hundred profit. Coz Henry has been up to see mother & said she promised to pay that note but wanted me to pay the interest. I asked him where the money was that the place rented for. I thought that was to pay the interest. I told you before I came away that if those calves bothered to sell them. Do the cows hold out milk

25

pretty well? Did you get the money on County Order? You can expect to draw your monthly due at any time you wish. Also that road order will come around soon. I have asked you twice how much money that was that John brought. I wanted to make a note of it. You have twice told me you got it all right but are very careful not to say how much. It is no matter now. I only mention it as a reminder that I like to have the figures. Do you have to tie up the cow? Where did Alex fix the calve pen? I am interested in all the little particulars. We have our incidents here such as a man being shot for trying to run the guards, etc. but it has not that particular interest of home incidents. Hope Amanda will not have a course of fever & ague. Hope she will learn that she is subject to natures laws & that such triumphs are accomplished by commencing gradually & regularly. We have some frost & ice here on the watering troughs. Hope the babes are well don't let them run out in the country air. We have rumors that we are soon off but I don't believe until I see.

Medicines available during the Civil War were limited.......other than the above mentioned aloe and rhubarb, quinine, morphine, and castor oil were offered as cures. Whiskey was accepted as medicinal and used as a prophylactic treatment. Patent medicines, usually containing a high amount of alcohol were also prescribed. There was a brisk black market for any of these substances.

Norwood did not survive the war to return home

June 11, 1863
Dear Sister,
Your letter came to hand yesterday. I never realized before how much sadness a few lines could bring – never. It all seems so like a dream I cant believe it true. How quickly would I have laid down my life if that dear one could have been spared. You say you do not feel rebellious, certainly then I must not. I have thought many times of what Mrs. H.

said of Albert soon after he left here. She had given him up to his country but not to die. More sad if possible would have been that morning parting had not hope sustained. I was sure he would be returned. Of course I was unprepared for such news. O God mourn other hearts the same? Bless God for the promise so they may be thrice blessed that you can claim it for yourself. Uncle went up to your fathers this morn. They had just received your letter. Thinking there will be no funeral sermon preached elsewhere we have concluded to have one a week from this PM. Pastor always improves every such occasion so well. He has taken such an interest in you all and Norwood was so well known here these are the reasons sufficient for justifying the occasion. Are they not? How I wish I was with you. I would not have come home if I had known all. I want to go there very much indeed. It seems as though I must when I think of it. Do not know but if I had the means in my purse I should start.

Daves funeral sermon is preached this morning the Baptist church. I did not feel like going out. After his company started from B. he came back there and was married. He started the next morn. Died in Hospital. You will receive other letters from here at the same time with this but we are not afraid of opening the wound afresh as it can not soon be healed. Two little darlings that will so often speak that one word Papa will soon forget him. May their heavenly father be more to them than an earthly parent possibly could. We feel very anxious to hear from you often. Do drop one if only a line to us. Or get someone to write for you. Do you know where Joseph's co. are now? I was very punctual to write until the time he commenced marching since which time we have been so anxious. Kiss the babes for me more than once and accept one for yourself. Your sister.

Very Dear Anna,
With quickened pulse and tearful eye I add a line. Uncle has
just returned from church & Rev. preached text, "all things
shall work together for good to those who love God etc."
may you dear Anna prove the truth of that blessed promise.
May you feel the power of this sustaining grace. It is painful
that none of the relatives are with you but God who takes
thought for the widow will not suffer you to lack friends or
comforts in your extremity. My heart bleeds for you but I
know you are a heroic woman and your faith will shame my
weaker self. When I first knew the contents of your letter a
chilling sensation about the hart came over me. It stooped
my breath nearly – no tears then – but now come tears both
breath and weep – blessed be tears. Your father had got your
letter this morning & said their team was not at home but
they would soon come here and see what could be done for
you. I suppose you could not consistently return this winter
nor do I know you wish to do so. I hope you will write every
particular which your friends ought to know. Glad am I you
have a mother to unburden your trials. Let us know your
feelings & circumstances. The Baptist church was quite full
and aged parents and young were mourning. Mr. W. has a
son in the Army who used to write often & had not heerd
from him in seven weeks & intends starting to hunt for him
tomorrow. We think he may be dead. Oh there is weeping in
almost every house.   Your Aunt

January 1863
My Darling Sister, how can I write? What shall I say? All
attempts at consolation seem almost a mockery in the first
overwhelming tide of sorrow. My heart is with you. It almost
forgets its own desolation in contemplating your greater
bereavement. Your breast has a double weight of sorrow you
realize not only your own loss but that of the dear little ones
added to it. May the everlasting arms of the almighty be
placed sound about you and his grace support you. Heaven

help us all in pain. Of him I dose not trust myself to speak. My heart bleeds afresh at every mention of his name…Norwood. Write often & tell me all the varied emotions of your heart which will find a ready sympathy and quick response.

Sabbath Morn Jan. 1863
My Dear Daughter, My mind and heart have been greatly drawn toward you and the dear little ones for several weeks past tho I did not know but your health was usually good until Amanda came home. Perhaps it was the thought that forces itself upon my mind that the sad intelligence we might at any time be called to hear, would fall with double weight on your heart. Knowing his constitution as I did & how much he suffered in consequence of exposure I hardly thought he would feel it to be his duty to offer his services – fearing they would not be efficient. Of course I was not prepared for the intelligence and spent many a night suffering for him and for the army. Yesterday morning Laura and Amanda went to the office. When they returned with the open letter – at a glance at their speaking countenances was sufficient to reveal its contents. You have heard so direct it must be so. All that was mortal of my dear boy – my only son – and your dear husband is entombed in his country's great grave yard. A fitting resting place perhaps could we put aside all selfish and regretful feelings. Did he not give himself up to his country? Now your little ones have two fathers in Heaven. Precious children may it be true. In your great sorrow you do not forget that we are not the only mourners in the land. They have commenced to return from the Baptist church. The funeral of Isaac has been attended there, or rather the services. The remains were brought back to be interred. He died in a hospital near New York City. Amanda has come perhaps she will finish this for me. My eyes are so dim. Your Mother

NEWS REPORT: *The Union News* 1864
One newspaper estimates that the number of destitute
widows and orphans, made such by the war in Virginia alone
is 60,000, and say they will mostly be a charge on public
charity, owing to the want of employment.

The end of the American Civil War left more than 620,000
soldiers dead. Statistics such as those mentioned above were
repeated in every state. The following certificate paid the
Widow White $124 for the loss of her husband, plus his $75
bounty payment.

ANNA ROSE
Not all those disabled by war were compensated. It was not
easy to obtain a Civil War Pension. Sidney Louis Rose, of
Pine Valley, New York enlisted in Co. B. 30th Pennsylvania
Militia Infantry for the "Emergency of 1863". According to

official government reports, and affidavits from friends,
Sidney was a strong and able bodied man when he enlisted.
While in camp with the regiment in Harrisberg, Pa.,"the
men were exposed in bad weather. Sidney suffered from
bronchitis and was troubled with severe diarrhea and piles
the size of chestnuts". The afflictions continued on the march
from Harrisburg to Carlile, Pennsylvania. The "trots" were
continuous throughout his time in service...the condition so
bad that when "Rose rushed to the woods the pickets did not
challenge his destination or reason". Sidney could not keep
up with the men of his unit on the march and was mustered
out of the Union Army with an honorable discharge after
only a little over one month of service. When he returned to
civilian life he resided in a boarding house owned by Mrs.
Pierce in Elmira. He shortly married another roomer, Anna
Wood. When Sidney applied for a disability pension the
physician affirmed to the government that Sindey was
entitled to ¼ disability for catarah, 1/8 for disease of the
liver and spleen, and ½ for extreme piles (hemeroids). All
legal documents attested that he was a talented wagon and
barrel maker whose health make work almost impossible –
one friend stated that when he did work he would need to
"grab his behind and try to poke the piles back inside as the
discomfort was acute". No pension was granted because he
did not serve the required 90 days. Sidney died in 1890, and
his widow Anna was left destitute. By 1907 she was still
living on public charity and friends once again appealed to
the government for assistance:

Pine Valley, New York   October 5, 1907
Commissioner of Pensions
Dear Sir, Will you kindly inform me what is the reason Anna
M. Rose of Pine Valley does not become entitled to a
widows pensions. She is a woman who can only live a short
time and is needy and as her husband Sidney L. Rose died
September 7, 1890 she has no support but charity. Sidney L.

Rose Co. B. 30th Reg. Pennsylvania. He died at this place. She has never married again. She married Sidney in July 1866 therefore she must be entitled to a widows pension. She once made application but could not find out why she did not become a pensioner. Will you kindly write me why or if there is any reasons why or if not send to her address at Pine Valley, Chemung Co., NY Please answer my letter so we can know.

Mrs. Althea B. Halpin

Attorneys were aggressive in efforts to assist, and exorbitantly charge, veterans and widows in obtaining their due from the government. The overly disputatious tactics led to the enactment of federal legislation limiting the price private attorneys could charge for representing veterans in claims and grievances against the US government. The five dollar fee made it almost impossible to obtain private legal council. This legislation remained in place virtually unchanged until 2006 when a new statute was enacted by the 109th congress to reform the antiquated law. The following ad placed by an attorney was in an 1863 newspaper.

THE NEW ENGLAND GUARDS
Company K – 44th Reg't. Mass. Volunteers.

This Regiment was a militia unit raised to fill the quota of Massachusetts and were mustered into the service in September. In October of 1862 the regiment headed for Beaufort, North Carolina on the steamer Merrimac, arriving at Morehead City, N.C. and immediately boarded a train for Newbern, N.C. The regiment then became part of Stevenson's Brigade...later part of the 2nd Brigade of Wessell's (4th) Division, Foster's (18th) Corps. They remained on duty until mustering out in June 1863

William Henry Lord *was a Sergeant in the 44th Massachusetts New England Guards. He wrote frequently to his family at home in West Roxbury, Massachusetts. West Roxbury is a suburban corner of Boston that was settled in 1630 and received its name because of the rocky geology of the region.*

Many of the following letters were written at a regimental hospital at Camp Stevenson in New Bern, North Carolina. The letters often ended ***"With a True God Bless".*** *In general, a stay in these medical units was almost a death sentence...cleanliness and medicines were nearly non existent, disease was rampant as was gangrene. Soldier Lord was pleased with his treatment, which included a supply of liquor. Fort Stevenson was located a little north of New Bern up the Neuse River.*

New Bern, North Carolina, *where Sgt. Lord was stationed, was founded in 1710 at the confluence of the Trent and Neuse rivers. It was a major port and trading center captured and occupied by the Union Army after a battle in March of 1862.*

CAMP STEVENSON – Newbern, N.C. Monday evening December 1862

My ever dear friend & mother, the first day of December you would hardly think its here in this state the weather has been very much like the weather we have at home in the later part of August or first of September. Comfortable without any overcoat on in the daytime but with one in the evening as it is quite a change rather damp & cold but not so unhealthy now as in the summer as we have had frost which makes the night air more healthy here. I have commenced a letter to you so as to have one ready to send by the next mail as we very often have only a short notice and so do not get much time to write – so in that I can give way to make more room for the other Sergts. I wish you would send me or have them send Sunday Herold's and cut out of the paper all accounts concerning the 44th all about our expedition. I hear that our Corporal has made a much larger story than what it really is. There was a letter in the Transcript about us from one of the Sergts. which I should like to read if you can get it without much trouble. I have received a few newspapers for which I am very much obliged. The 8th and 51st have arrived and the rumor is that they got short of rations & opened a lot of boxes that they thought belonged to QMasters but afterward proved to belong to the 44th (private boxes) now weather that is true is more than I can say or have found out. There was some boxes arrived here a few days ago but none for me as I had expected as they come by Adams Express. It is now most time for taps. I must make up my bed so good night. Since writing the above I have heard that there will be a mail or rather Mr. Barnard of Warren St. Chapel who is here will take a few letters on with him. He has two sons in this regiment. I have permission to write a few minutes after taps. Our orderly Sergt. received a letter from his mother this morning by a small mail that came by the 80th & 51st but there was none for me, it was a mail made up of letters that happened to be in Boston, all the mails go to NY now if you hear of Steamer that is to leave Boston for Newbern you can send letters by some of the officers as that has been done here. The orderleys' mother said that we had a very hard time of it. Some did I know But as for myself I stood it first rate and was never in better health then I was when I returned from the march & am now in first rate health. We had sufficient to eat as most every town we stopped at we shot pigs & were et up & on the march on two legs in a very short time. I had plenty of turkeys, chickens, geese, pigs, fresh beef honey, preserves, water, coffee & numerous other eatables that I can not stop now to mention but do not fear but what I shall have enough to eat as I always look out for number one in that pretty well as you well know by experience. I hope to return to you all in about six months, the rebs will soon be gone and you will see me safe and sound. There has a man just come here to the door & says that another mail has arrived & that a man has gone down to the city to get it now weather he gets it in time for us before this letter goes I can not say. There had aught to be a lot of letters for me as there is several mails due here. I will write by every mail if it is only half a dozen lines, so do not think I neglect you. I have thus far only received two letters from you & one from Mr. & Mrs. Smith that is all the letters I have. So you must think I should wish to hear from home. I shall wait faithfully for them as I feel there are some on the way for me. Give my love to the Wilcoxes, Wescotts, & your neighbors I think of them very often & of the many good times we have all had together. How I should like to go into the dining room & get an apple to eat. We have to pay 5 cts. for two & 40 cts. a pound for butter, 20 cts. lb. for cheese. Can not buy anything here for less than 5 cents. 5 cents for this, five cents for that. I had a pair of pants washed 5 cts., shirt 5 cts., same for drawers & handkerchiefs. We do not see white collars very often. I am to have a mattress tomorrow, I also have two nice woolen blankets (which is one more than the men have) & my overcoat but I find my

blankets sufficient to keep me warm. You must write often &
oblige your most affect. Son, With a true God BlessYou,
good night. Wm. Henry Lord
There was no mail arrived here last night, false alarm, the 8th
& 51st had a rough passage.

This drawing of Camp Stevenson, NC was included with the soldier's letter.

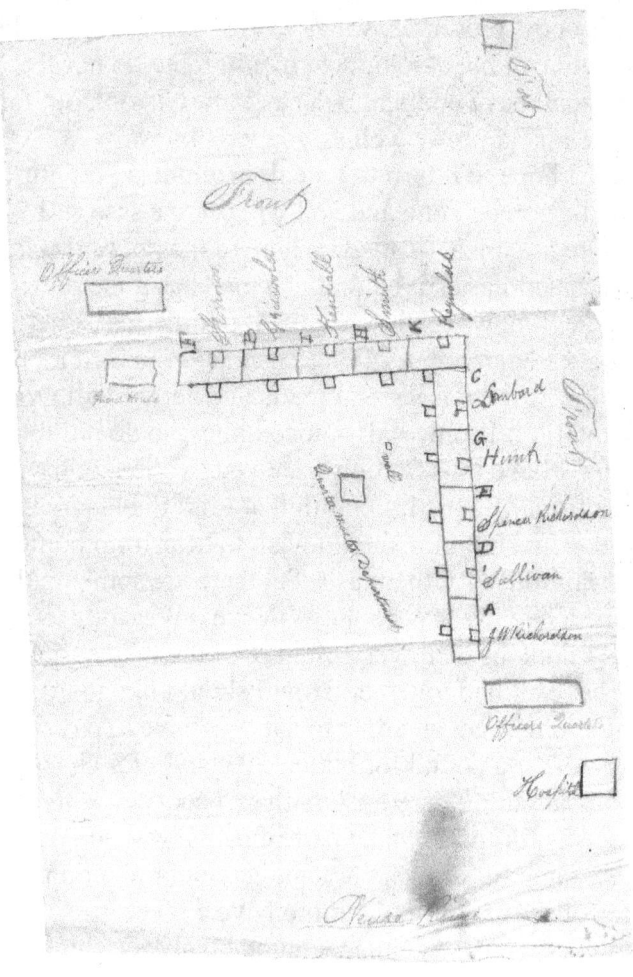

New England Guards - New Bern, N.C., Dec.1872 Letter #15
Ever Dear Mother, excuse this scribbling as I am sitting up in bed down to the hospital sick with the back door trots. Was taken yesterday morning but am a great deal better, now my bones ache considerable and the surgeon thought he could take great deal better care of me here than he could at camp. Now do not be worried about me I am in charge of good hands & shall be soon back to my regiment. The box of condensed milk with jug of pickles arrived yesterday in good order for which I am much obliged. My boots have not yet arrived. The mail was here tonight but I shall not write much. I shall soon be better so do not worry too much about your soldier boy. I have got a cold in my head which uses me up the most, my back door trots is a great deal better today than it was pretty bad yesterday. I shall not be able to write to the Smiths by this mail & if they see yours you must excuse me so also my other friends.
Placing my trust in God, I remain your most affectionate son, with a True God Bless You – Wm. Henry Lord.

PS - My back is all right but I wish you would send me a small 1863 almanac, two or three of them if you can get them. I have written the facts in regard to my sickness so do not think I misrepresented it to you. I have forgotten the number of this letter as my ap. book being up camp. Yours, WHL

NEW ENGLAND GUARDS – 44th Regt. Mass. Volunteers
Newbern, N.C. December 1862 - letter # 16
Ever Dear Mother, you may number my last of the 27th instant no.15, as I did not have my books with me then, since writing my last I have been rather more sick. Saturday night the Dr. gave me some medicine to throw off the bile on my

stomach as I found out since that I was threatened with the Bilious Fever. Had enough of it that night as I was going up & down most all the later part of the night. Had severe pain in my lungs for the past day or two & have had since Monday morning. I woke from a restless nights rest getting up & coughing most all the night, when Dr. Ware came he sounded *(listened to lung sounds by placing ear on chest)* me as he had done several times before & then cupped me taking about a half cup full of blood from my back just under my left shoulder blade, no doubt to resolve the pain in my lungs & I think now that it was a help in a certain degree, although not much.

Tuesday morning, have had a poor night rest but have had a good days rest & have written up my diary, was over a week behind which was quite a job for me. Wed. The last day of the year had a splendid night rest sleeping most all night & coughing very little & woke feeling first rate & rested. Capt. Reynolds has just been in to see me he has resigned & is going home in the next Steamer & he will call & see you soon after his arrival. He said that he was to be near WR or in it, I suppose that will be in according to his health. I intend sending this letter by him also a second letter & another paper with a picture all taken of Kinston when I last visited that place, you will find his name by taking out the picture from the frame. I shall not write any more tonight as I am getting tired.

Thursday – Jan. 1, 1863 – Had a fair nights rest, coughed a little, the pain in my lungs is not quite so severe I think but I have a severe pain in my left side, it is very singular that my back does not trouble me when I was lamed a few years ago, but is it all right & tight. Capt. Reynolds has sent over for this once this morning & I did not have it ready so you must excuse me for not writing more. Hoping you are well with much love to you ever dear and kind parents I remain your most affectionate son Wm. Henry Lord

PS: This letter is hardly worth the trouble for Capt. Reynolds to go the house with but I know that you would like to see him as he is direct from me, so I think that will make up for my not writing more. I send you a stamp & picture of Rebels from string, be careful when you take the picture out of the frame as I have got the stamp there.

String Art – *a camp craft, pictures made by soldiers during rest periods*
Bilious Fever – *interpreted as intestinal fever or malaria*
During the many hours of waiting for action enlisted men often resorted to games of chance for entertainment. These **playing cards** *were actually used by a soldier of the Civil War. No numbers were used on the cards.*

Cupping *was a standard remedy for decades before, during and after the Civil War. Many homes had their own set of "cups" for emergency treatment. Although the job could be done with a standard glass tumbler, the medical jars were very heavy glass with a round bottom each about 2 inches tall. Both Dry and Wet cupping procedures were used.*

Dry cupping consisted of moistening the inside of several cups with alcohol or whiskey which was then lighted and applied at once to the part of the anatomy to be treated. As the air in the glass cooled it would "suck" the blood and " ill humors" to the surface of the skin, due to the contraction of the air...thus causing large red blisters.

Wet cupping was a bit messier than dry, requiring preparation of the skin by the dry cupping method and then making parallel incisions in the skin and placing hot cups over the area again. The cups would fill with blood to be removed along with "troublesome elements". It is understandable that the mother of this soldier was not fond of the cupping cure.

Dozens of glass cups were usually part of a physicians and home medical kits. Pictured below are two, each with a heavy rounded bottom, suitable for being heated.

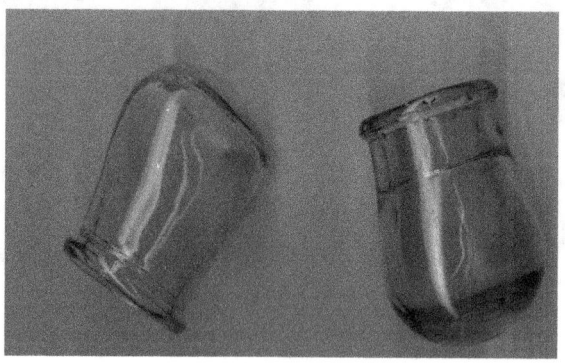

N. C. Dec. 1862 - letter # 17
Ever Dear Mother, I shall not write but a few lines to send
you my mail as I intend sending a letter by Capt. Reynolds
who is going home having resigned his commission on
account of ill health, he will call & see you soon perhaps
before this reaches you. If he does not see you before you
will know that it is because he is fatigued by the voyage &
will as soon as he is able. He expects to leave tomorrow or
the next day - we are sorry to part with him. I am very, very
sorry to loose him as a Captain - he was kind hearted, ever
obliging & kind toward us all, willing to do his best by all &
we shall miss him more now that we know we have lost him
for the rest of the time in service. I hardly know now who
will be Capt. But hope we shall get a good one but I do not
wish for a better man than Capt. Reynolds has been to us. I
send much love to all & a goodly share to your own dear
self. I am getting better slowly & am in good hands. Dr.
Ware, son of old Dr. Ware has charge of me & our Reg. &
he knows his business, and the men he has under his charge
here at the hospital like him much & have full confidence.
Give my love to all enquiring friends & they must excuse me
for not writing as it is hard work for me when I am laying
down. Hoping to hear from you soon & very often I remain
your most affect. Son Wm. Henry Lord.
PS: I received a letter from Mr. S. tonight but am not able to
write also one from Nat & Blossus a week ago but am not
able to answer any of them.

North Conway, N.H. November 1863
From Rebecca - My dear friends, I know that your welcome letter aught to have been answered before this but one thing after another has prevented my doing so. We have had very exciting times here for seven or eight weeks past with the *draft and then the fires*. I suppose you have heard all about it. Most of the conscrypts felt rather bad but I believe they made no resistance in this town, all paid that did not get exempt without, none has gone. I suppose you have seen an account of the Jackson Riot in the papers. And then we have had the fires to trouble us and we feel that we are not safe at all. It is supposed that these incendiaries are lurking around here now. Mr. Eastmans barns and Mortons that were burned were at Conway Center and Mr. Mudgetts house and barn was, that large boarding house close by the gate where we went in to go to the Willey burying ground. They lost besides the house and barns 40 tons of hay 2 good horses a yolk of oxen 5 cows 6 hogs besides a great deal of furniture and clothing his loss is estimated at $3,000 or $4,000 and besides this they have been robbing clothes lines on the other side of the river from us, they have taken whole washings. How is it with you? Do you have any such troubles? How do you all do? I was very sorry to hear you had such bad colds but you are well now. Has Mrs. Thompson got well and finaly how are all our friends in Concord & Pembroke? We are at present as swell as usual except as the cold whether come on. Mother begins to be troubled with the neuralgia. The folks at the other house are about the same as usual. Grandmother appears about the same as when I last wrote you. She has been over here 2 or 3 times the past week but she is so changed there is but little satisfaction in seeing her. She is a poor pitiful creature. They have been at work on their house this fall. Have raised the old part a story and a half so it is two story and a half now. The old chimney taken down, two new ones built go up stairs in the front entry and all fixed over, painted white outside. Next Thursday is

Thanksgiving and I wish you could come and spend it with us. I think we could have a good time, anyway we would try. I often think of my visit at your house and how glad I would be to go again but I shall have to wait a while. I think of going to Portland and around this winter if nothing happens to prevent it. It is almost dinner time and I must close. We all send lots of love to you all and wish we could see you. Also remember us to enquiring friends. When did you hear from aunte? Hoping this will find you all well & you will write soon with all the news. From your affectionate friend, Rebecca. We has had some pictures taken and thinking you would like one you will find it enclosed. How do you like it?

The great Civil War draft riots were a grave problem incited by the Union Conscription Act of March 3, 1863. The largest revolts were centered in New York City, but violence broke out in many other Northern states, including New Hampshire, where this letter was written. Blacks, abolitionists and those wealthy enough to purchase an exemption were all targets for attack, and so were random businesses and clotheslines.

Draft riots continued throughout the following year as reported in the *Union, NY News* **in September, 1864:**
"In Sunbury, Pa. a newspaper called the *American,* states that one thousand citizens , determined to resist the draft, collected near that place, some time since, and entrenched themselves on a mountain. Gen. Couch sent an expedition after them, and they surrendered to it. What became of them is not stated."

Newbern, N.C. – January 8, 1863 – letter #18
Ever Dear Mother – I know you will feel anxious because
you do not hear from me but there has no mail left Newbern
since I wrote last which was Sat. the 31st of December, it
seems an age almost since I have written & do not know now
when there is one that goes but thought I would write so as to
be ready when there is a mail. My health is now a great deal
better. I have been out today for the first time since I sent
into the Hospital. The first few days I was very sick with a
touch of *the lung fever* and my left lung is now quite sore.

Friday 9th of January – Have been out today & am going to
try to get a ride up to camp to make the boys a visit of a few
hours. I shall not probably go on the next expedition
although I want to very much. There is a large expedition to
start from here in a few days, there are forty thousand troops
here at Newbern and vicinity and it will be a big thing. The
Monitor was sunk off Hateras on its way to Newbern. There
was another Moniter with her, a larger one than the original
Moniter that was sunk, it has arrived here probably to take
part in the great expedition. The general opinion is that they
are going to Wilmington, N.C. while others think Charleston,
S.C. is their destination but we shall have to wait and time
will tell. It is a great disappointment to me that I can not go
but I suppose that it is all for the best. I know that you will
feel happy to think I can not go but I want to go with the 44th
wherever it goes no matter what the danger is & never want
to be left behind and am willing to share the danger and
hardships with the rest of the boys. I am much obliged for
the contents of the box & thank you kindly for the paper. I
can obtain of the Chaplain as nice and as cheap as you can
get it in Boston so do not trouble yourself to send more.
There was a tear on top it had commenced to decay a little
but I eat what was good of it. I did not take all the things out
of the box so do not know what else there was. I told the

44

Sergts. to look out for it and I suppose they have tasted of those finer things as I am not being able to eat them but could eat them now if I had the chance at them. I will not write more now but will before the mail closes. I intend buying a bottle of ink today so that you will be able to read my letters better. I have been obliged to write with a pencil since being in the hospital and in bed. Hoping to hear from you soon & with much love to you & family I remain your affect. Son Wm. H. Lord

(I have not a chance to write as this goes by private conveyance and am now better able to be out – Jan. 11.)

Lung Fever – Pneumonia

The following drawing of **iron clad vessels** *was probably removed from an old book.*

THE REBEL IRON-CLAD FLEET FORCING THE OBSTRUCTIONS IN JAMES RIVER.—[Sketched by A. R. Waud.]

The great iron clad fighting ships were propelled by steam and fitted with iron plates of armor. Many styles of ironclads were used, for deep water and inland waterways. The costal monitors were for use in sheltered waters and rivers. The most well known, Monitor, went to sea in 1862, and battled to a draw the previously invincible Confederate ship Merrimac (renamed the Virginia). The Monitor sank off Cape Hatteras during a gale.

Monitor – a class of Ironclad produced by Union forces

NEWS REPORT: December 1863
The monitor Weehawken sunk at her moorings off Morris Island, S.C. on Sunday last, during the prevalence of a gale. Thirty of her crew perished among whom were four of her engineers. The Captain and remainder of the officers are safe. The other monitors rode out the storm.

Newbern, N.C. – Jan. 15, 1863 – letter # 19
My Ever Dear Mother, I hope ere this that you have received some of my letters and seen my Capt. There has a mail arrived and I am expecting letters down every minute. My health is better a little, than it was when I wrote to you last but my left lung is quite sore also my right but not as much as the left. I go out every day and what is most singular we had not had a storm for a month or 6 weeks. Have had several showers for a few hours but nothing lasting. Your kind welcome letters of Dec. 29th & Jan. 1st have just come down from camp. I have had great pleasure in reading them. It is now most 4 weeks since I have received any letters the mails are very irregular and we do blow off considerable sometimes because we do not get more letters but we live on and hope for the best and trust that every day we shall have a mail. I will now answer your # 8 but may not get through with it before I may hastily close as I expect *Mr. Bond of*

Boston the watch and clockmaker in and he will forward it much sooner than by the regular mail.
William Bond & Sons was a business of Boston renowned for decades as silversmiths, clock makers and astronomers.
I thank you for your Merry Christmas, had a very good time but did not feel very smart *(well)* as I have already written you. You must not My Dear Mother worry so much about me. God will watch over and protect me whether I am on the battle field or in my barrack which I now call my home. I am sorry Elizabeth is so unhappy since her dear Ben has been away and hope that all the friends that the soldiers have left at home are not going to be unhappy as it will only make us feel all the worse and we all know that we feel bad enough about being away from dear ones left at home…the dearest spot on earth. There is not much chance for an enlisted man to make much money here as Col. Kurtz has died.

The officers high in office as he was stand a much better chance. There are about 1/8 or ¼ of our regiment or brigade so that they do not have to do military duty but they have to have influential friends to get them. Now I suppose you wish that I might get detailed but there is no chance so, do not hope for it as it is no use. I do not think we shall be beaten by the Rebs although they fight well when they are strongly fortified and know how to run full as well as our troops do sometimes, that was an awful battle at Fredericksburg only to think that the same number should be lying on the field dead and wounded as we had in our last expedition, it makes me think sometimes.

By the time the battle in Fredericksburg in December of 1862 ended many thousands of Union soldiers were wounded and dead on the battlefield. Medical help was not available until the next day…the delay contributed to further deaths.

47

I am glad that the girls had a surprise party and hope as no doubt they did have a nice time & should liked to have shared it with them. A Christmas box would have been very acceptable. The cakes & pies came in good shape, a nice plumb pudding would go bad, they do not open the boxes although they have a right to do so. There is a fellow that sleeps in the bed beside me that is to have a shoe box full of extras come to him & it is on the way. You say you are glad I am not on the Potomac, I am of the same opinion as your own dear self on that subject. Dr. Draper is a surgeon in the army, it almost makes me sick to think of it, him a regular old "sawbones" not fit to dress a wound or take charge of a sick man. I am glad and thankful that there is no chance of my being under his charge. I am happy to hear that Mr. Gilbert Clark has got money enough to live upon and hope he will not be unfortunate and lose it, although I should not object to some of it. That is the big thing, the change in S.C. Gookin & Co.s establishment there is no doubt but what they will keep my place open for me, at least I shall not worry much about it at present. No.8 being finished I will proceed with your # 9. You are very fortunate in receiving my letters on Holidays, you say you received my two letters on New Years Day, you are more fortunate than myself as I have not received any on such days, but am glad enough to get them any day.

Friday Jan. 11. – Last night after I had gone to bed & got to sleep I was aroused by somebody putting something near my head, it proved to be a young man from camp with two letters for me that had come by a second mail. I was not sorry I had been aroused and I immediately got a candle & went to reading, one was from yourself and the other from George. I will now proceed with No. 9. Do not doubt that you would be perfectly willing to keep my suppers for me and put up my dinners as for the latter I hope I shall be

48

obliged to carry my dinner as it is a great bother and you know I never liked it much. I shall not go on the next expedition and probably shall not again for a great while. I have let you know the worst as far as I can, there are so many little things not worth mentioning that we all forget when we sit down to write home that we do not think them of any account. I stood the fatigue as well as the best of them and kept with my company which a great many of the Sergents did not do. Sergt. Emery of Co. H gave out on the first expedition and also on the second day of the last one. Now I know you will think I had aught to write about them but there is no use for me to go into the little details. You ask how I felt when I went into Battle, it did not trouble me much, not half so much as it has to go some places in Massachusetts, of course if a fellow thought of home and that there was a chance of getting or catching a small piece of lead. But I was more particular to try and give them a part of the contents of my cartridge box, but have no more fears as there is not much danger for me for a long while. You ask if I did not tremble, no nairy a tremble and I was anxious to give it to them. We could not bear to see our comrades wounded. That is a big thing. *Dan Long's present* I should not at all object to giving. I am glad to hear that you all had a good time at George's Christmas and should have had no objections to have been there. What do you mean about there being a great many changes before the 4th of July? In what respect do you mean in regard to home affairs or what, please let me know in your next letter. I have not had a chance yet to go and see Theodore since my return but have heard from him by way of men in his company. He was well, his camp is about 3 or 4 miles from ours and I have not yet felt able to walk there. Please do not say you are ashamed of your writing. I have no trouble at all reading them so please write often no matter if it is only a half dozen lines, they are received with great pleasure. Friends at home can not write to often to suite me. I will proceed with no. 10. I have not exposed myself any more than I could help and took just as good care of your youngest son as circumstances would permit. I should like to have had my flask filled on the last expedition with whiskey or brandy but did not, as I emptied it on the first expedition and had a chance to fill it before I left but the price was rather high and I thought it would not pay, but I am all right on that score now. Dr. Ware give me a quart bottle of whiskey and I shall look out and save enough to fill my flask to keep for a case of emergency. There is no need of my getting my "discharge" at present I am not sick enough for that and Dr. Ware said yesterday afternoon that I should probably be all right in three or four weeks. It would be poor policy for me to come home now or in a month or two on account of the cold weather you are having and will have for some time to come, as great change would be too much for me & I should be likely to take cold on my lungs. I am comfortably situated here and have good care, plenty of bed clothes, I have got new four nice warm woolen blankets and could have more if I needed them but I throw off a part of them at times as I am so warm. The weather here is quite warm and is like one of our June days. You must see that it would not be good policy for me to come home at this changeable season in the North. I shall get well much quicker to remain here. My lungs are getting stronger every day & I shall soon be well, walk out every day & gaining strength so do not worry. I shall look out for No. 1 as well as the best of them as that is the game here in the Army and I am learning to trade very fast. You will hardly be able to take charge of me when I get home, you will take us all for fast boys, always hungry in the best of living and looking out for the best tit bits for no. 1. My box will be received in a very few days as the steamer has arrived and is waiting to unload. I am very much obliged to you and all that helped fill the box please thank them for me. The box will be very acceptable just at the present time and I shall enjoy it hugely. I will most certainly let you know when I receive it. I will not go into details to thank them personally for the contents so you will thank them well for the deed. Perhaps I may in my next letter, or when the box is received. I am very much obliged to Eva & Everett for their kiss and will send them a heap in return, tell them to come out here and see me so that I can trot them upon my knee as I used to. I am glad that you did not send a turkey as it would have spoiled. There have been a great many sent and they have all spoiled. You need not feel bad & think the rest will all be mush, the pies & cakes come out here in first rate shape and this coming so quick can not help being nice. I have received my boots. You say you do not like *cupping,* it did not hurt much and was not at all sore after, anyway I was willing to have him do what he wished with me as I placed full confidence in him. I think he brought me up very quick. I had a regular run of fever and am now getting along & improving first rate. Remember me to Benj. when any of you write. I do not know what his regiment is. I should like to know very much. Give my love to Mrs. Seaver. Now I think your very kind and welcome letters answered. You must be tired of reading but some how or other I have run on and could not seem to stop writing. I am in just the mood today, but when I started I thought I should not write more than four pages. It is most night now and I shall not write more. The letters I received from George, Janet & Lizzie I may not answer by this mail although I shall try to. I want to go up to camp tomorrow and I shall not have much time if the mail goes tomorrow as there is a rumor to that effect. My lungs are a great deal better today than yesterday to my great surprise. I will write tomorrow but now must close as it is quite dark. Give my love to my brothers & sisters and all enquiring friends also a good share to your own dear self. Hoping to hear from you soon and very often and with a True God Bless I remain your most affectionate son. W. Henry Lord

Dan Long's present – *refers to a long rifle and the present of a lead ball or bullet*

The tin type picture shows a soldier with a typical long rifle.

Sat. 17th – I nearly overlooked what you write about Col. Lee's cruelty to his men – about his threatening to shoot those who did not keep up. Now that is not so in regard to those who were not able to keep up account of fatigue, but he

DID threaten to shoot some that did not obey his orders. Now I was nearby when it happened & will explain. There was a ford, or crick, that we were obliged to pass through. Now there are a great many fords & places we can not walk over and keep our feet dry, but there was no chance of our doing so and there were some that tried to keep their feet dry. The Col. ordered them forward and they still continued to pick their way even when there was no use as our feet were doomed to be wet in that ford, half up to our knees. When he drew his pistol & they went on he would not have dared to fire, neither did the men that he aimed at think so, but they do like to make up a large story to send home. Those few kept all the men in the rear behind & making them double quick to catch up again with the advance. It provoked me to read some of the corporal's letters in the Herald. He makes out to large a story about some things that he has no right to and it provoked the other boys considerable.

I am better this morning and intend going up to camp today. Do not worry any more about our Col. He looks out for us and takes good care of his men first rate. He goes ahead of a great many other Col.s here and I am glad and thankful that I am not in any other regiment and I am perfectly contented with Col. Lee. I am improving every day and hope will soon be well. Do not feel bad about me there is no need of my getting a discharge at present and if I think it necessary to get it, bye & bye I will do so but it would be dangerous for me to return home now for a month or two as I said before. Much love as ever. WHL

Letter # 20 – Stanley Hospital, Newbern, N.C. – Jan. 19, 1863 – evening
Ever Dear Mother, I shall not write much to night as it is getting quite late, I have written to George & Frank & have been up to camp to day and have walked up & back for the past week except for one day it rained. I am getting quite strong now my lungs are better. My dear mother I fear that

you are unwell and worry too much about me. Have no fear I shall return home safe to you at the end of my term of service. I shall not go on the next expedition as you might suppose. Cheer up my dear & kind mother. The girls must excuse me for not writing to them but I have not time. Your box was received by me last Saturday with much pleasure. I opened it & put the letter in my pocket so as to eat some of the contents for dinner & was in a hurry to eat. I never thought of the letter until I put my hand into my pocket Monday morning & was provoked that I should have forgotten it. The contents of the box were in first rate order, except the hard ginger-bread sent by Louise that softened and I think had not better send any more of that. Your rounds were all right & the rest in good shape & I am greatly obliged to you and all that put anything in it. The sausages were bang up and tasted of home, so does the rest. Give my love to all. I must close now as it is late for writing. Turkeys are not very good when they get here. I am short of paper the reason I do not write more. Direct as before, a True God Bless – Wm. Henry

Bang up – *very good*

Number 21 – Newbern, N.C. – January 20, 1863
Dear Mother, I sent the letter of yesterday by a Mr. Biggs of So. Boston, No. 20, but I think I forgot to number it. Please do it for me. He will get to Boston much quicker than the mail that is going to night. I have nothing particular to write, nothing new here. The expedition has
not started yet and I do not know when it will go. You must excuse this short note. I am better and gaining every day and shall be very careful about going out so as not to take cold. Our company had an election 1st Friday evening & elected Lieut. Weld Capt. & Lieut. Brown as 1st Lieut., and Sergeant Parkinson as 2nd Lieut., they will all get their commissions. I shall remain here at the hospital until I get pretty strong and

not go on duty for some weeks to come. Do not worry I am more comfortable where I am than I would be at the barracks until my health is recovered. I sent twenty one dollars to Frank by Mr. Biggs thinking it would be safer to send it so than it would by mail. I must close now with much love to all and a True God Bless. I remain your affect. Son Wm. Henry Lord

This is a dry place for news at present. I will try to write a letter to Mr. Welch before the mail closes if I can. Time is short. Cheer up and please send me if you have a chance any way without much trouble my *fancy cap* that Mrs. Smith made for me, be sure & have it come dry.

Fancy Cap - It was a tradition with many military units for soldiers to wear fancy "camp caps" when not on duty. The chapeaus were usually home made and colorful knit creations. Pictured are soldiers wearing "Fancy caps".

No. 22 – Stanley Hospital, Newbern, N.C. Thurs. Jan. 22, 1863

Ever Dear Mother, have just heard that there was a mail going to night, it is now late in the afternoon and I shall not be able to write a great deal as I am obliged to send it to the office. My health is now better I think, improving every day, have a good appetite and have enough to eat, the boys here in the hospital all say I am growing fat. We have not had a pleasant day since Monday so have remained indoors, wishing that it would clear away and be nice so I could go out to walk, have a pass to any part of the city and in fact am a gentleman at large in Uncle Sam's service and have a first rate time am enjoying myself all I can. Do not worry about Sergt. Lord he will soon be well and hearty. I am first rate except my lung is a little sore yet. I have written to Lizzie, Jenny and one to Ella Smith which you may forward when you get a chance. If you send me another box while I am in the service you had better not send any meat as it will be rather warm and they will not likely to keep. I suppose my first box remained in the office a long while, that sailing vessel that was sent out by the Gentlemen of Boston hurried the express company up. I am very much obliged to you and will return the compliment when you enlist and go off to war. Remember me to all the neighbors and friends and give my love to all at home. With a True God Bless.

No. 23 – Newbern, N. C. Wednesday afternoon, January 23, 1863

Dear Mother, I have nothing particular to add my lungs are stronger. I shall not have time to write to my sisters as I have been writing to Mr. Welch. The mail goes tonight.
Remember me to encouraging friends. Much Love from your Wm. Henry

This letter was written on the back of scrap paper in the form of a blank note from the Newbern Bank.

No. 24 – New England Guards – Co. K – 44th Regt. Mass.
Volunteers – Feb. 3, 1863 – Stanley Hospital, Newbern
Ever Dear Mother, there is a mail close here tonight and I
will write you a few lines. Our regiment with two companies
of cavalry and ten pieces of marine artillery have gone on a
small expedition to Plymouth, N.C. the place where we went
on board of the transports on our return from Tarboro
expedition what the object in going is I do not know. They
have taken ten days rations with them. You will be gratified
to learn that your soldier boy has not gone with them. I went
out to see them Sunday morning as they passed by. It made
the tears come to my eyes after they passed by and left me
behind. I was sorry enough not to be with them. I had rather
be in battle or on the march than to be in a Hospital but am
comfortable situated as I am but I shall be glad when I can
rejoin the boys again. I have a pass to go to Beaufort it is
about 40 or 50 miles distant & shall go in a few days. Last
night about twelve or one o'clock we had a thunder shower
but it turned into snow and snowed until noon. It is now late
in the afternoon and the snow has most all disappeared. We
have had very warm weather and by tomorrow we shall have
a good warm day again. You will oblige me by delivering or
forwarding the enclosed letters to Louise and Martha. I am
now gaining every day but slowly. My last letter No. 23
dated Jan 23, should have been the 28th so excuse the
mistake. The health of our regiment is better now. Give my
love to all at home and remember me to the neighbors. God
bless you and make you happy and contented while I am
absent. Ever your true son, Wm. Henry Lord

Beaufort, N.C. *– When Union forces took Beaufort they found a
ghost town...all the white population had left and the slaves were
looting the town. General Stevens restored order and the small
village became a popular place for soldiers recovering from
wounds.*

No. 26 – Stanley Hospital, Newberg, N.C. Feb. 11, 1863
Ever Dear Mother, your very welcome letter of the 1st & 5th
numbers 14 & 15, were received this afternoon with great
pleasure. You say that Addie has written to me, I have not
received it. You must have forgotten to enclose it. I have
another pass in my pocket to go to Beaufort with a friend in
the Regiment and intend going tomorrow morning and
returning the next day. Am going to visit *Fort Macon* in the
afternoon. That is the reason I am writing so to have a letter
to go the next mail. It is a pleasure excursion, just a little trip
for my health. I am improving and getting to be pretty
strong. Ha Ha. Am happy to hear you sent another box,
anything from home is welcome. I expect to receive it soon
as there is a steamer arrived. Orderly Wild is an *old Betty*
and is not liked by the company or any of the officers in Co.
K. The men call him Aunt Betty, we all dislike him very
much but keep mum about it please. That is the reason Sergt.
Parkinson was put in over him. You need not worry about
my being dissatisfied with your cooking when I come home.
The *niggers* are not such nice cooks. There is a great
difference in them but none of them cook to suit me as well
as my mother. It is a little singular that I do not receive the
letters sent by Nate. Give my love to him if you see him, also
my love to all that may inquire for me and to all the family. I
must close now with much love I remain your most affect.
son in haste. Wm. Henry Lord

The word nigger, *of course, is not correct to use today but was
common during the Civil War era.*

OLD BETTY *– old fussbudget, with "odd tendencies"*

Fort Macon, North *Carolina was built in the 1820's of brick and
stone for the purpose of guarding the Beaufort Inlet and the
Beaufort Harbor. Two days after the Civil War began the North
Carolina Militia seized Fort Macon and installed 54 cannons. The*

Union forces recaptured the fort in1862 by laying siege and breaching the masonry walls.

THIS MAP SHOWS MANY OF THE LOCATIONS MENTIONED IN THE LETTERS

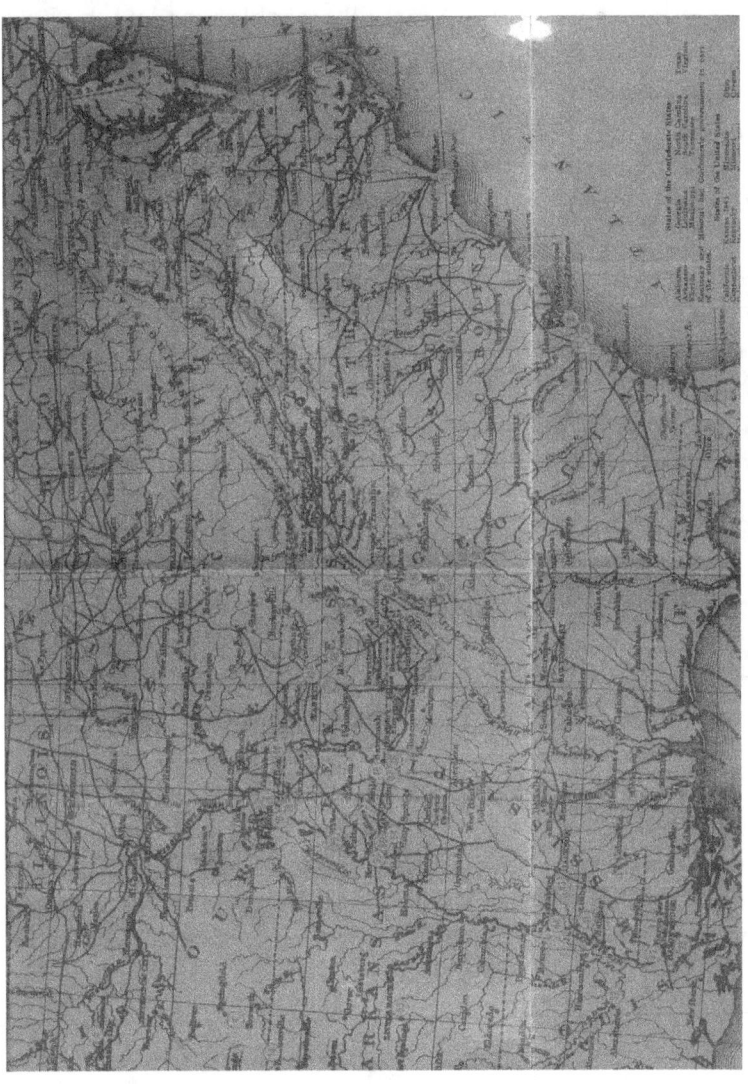

Letter No. 27 – Beaufort, N.C. – Ocean House – Thursday Evening – Feb. 12, 1863
Dear Mother, if you were to call to see your baby boy you would find him in room no. 14, setting in a chair at a table before a nice wood fire. You will probably wonder why I am here and not on a fighting expedition. But the thinking is the city of Beaufort by the sea shore forty miles distant might do me good. I got a pass for myself and a friend that I got acquainted with while I was sick, Charles L. Le Cain, and a fine fellow he is as far as I have seen. We left Newbern this morn on a train that was to start at nine but did not until ten, arrived at Morehead City, sailed over to Beaufort in a sail boat and arrived there at one, took dinner over at the hotel then sailed to Fort Macon where our forces had a battle last March. It is a very strong fort but the Rebs could not hold it. I will give you the particulars of this visit at a future day. We examined the fort and returned to our hotel where I shall remain until tomorrow noon then I shall return to Newbern. Beaufort is not much of a place, if it was in New England we should consider it a very small sized town, yet it is one of the healthiest places on the Southern Coast and much resorted to by the Nabobs. We have come to the conclusion we shall probably have beds enough tonight as there are three in the room & we will be sleeping together. The furniture consists of two chairs, one wash stand, a table, looking glass, three pitchers, half a dozen tumblers and several so fourths. We are to have a nice hot whiskey punch by Le Cain & Lord that will undoubtedly be very nice. I have thus far enjoyed my visit very much, we are two jolly good fellows and bound to be slightly warmed up before we retire. It is now quite late & I will bid you good night from your ever true, Wm. H. Lord.

Nabob – slang for wealthy people – the gentry

Newbern, Feb. 3, 1863
Have arrived home, am first rate, had a good time. My box
arrived safe and in good order. This goes by private
conveyance very soon, in great haste, yours, WHL

No. 29 – Camp Stevenson, Newbern, N. C. Feb. 18, 1863
Ever Dear Mother, the last letter I wrote to you I was at
Beaufort and had added a post script here at Newbern at my
barracks, that night I came up from the Hospital and happy I
am to be back again with very good health. I am now a great
deal better & think my trip to Beaufort done me good
although for a short time. I have written four letters today to
Father who I have not written to personally before, although
I suppose he has read my letters to Lizzie, Addie and Jennie.
I have not got much news to write to you by this mail. I am
almost well, have been excused for a walk. We have had our
room enlarged making it nearly twice as large as before, a
larger window put in to give us more light. We have had two
rainy days but have been busy all the time fixing up our
room. How are you getting along at home now, have you
clothes enough and do you have any money to spend now,
does father have work all the time so that he can provide for
you? Please write me and let me know the true facts how you
are situated. I am much obliged to you for sending those
handkerchiefs and my cap. They will do just swell to wear
out here but if I was coming out again I should have silk
ones, the niggers do not wash to suit me or in fact do
anything. But we are obliged to put up with them. Don't you
think it would be a good plan to have me send home my
washing. Our Col. is acting Brigadier General. General
Stevenson is away on the expedition and Lee is taking his
place in command of the remainder of the Brigade. I have
nothing more of interest to write and I will bid you good
night from your most affect. son, Wm. H. Lord

New England Guards Co. K – 44th Regt. – Mass. Volunteers
– Camp Stevenson, Newbern, N. C. – Feb. 18, 1863
Dear Father, Having about made up my mind that you will
not write to me unless I wrote you first I now take this
opportunity to write you a few lines. First of all promising
you that you will not obtain much news from this part of the
United States unless it is that Gen. Foster has left the great
expedition off Charleston, S. C. having had some trouble
with Gen. Hunter in regard to who should have command.
Gen. H. claiming that he had because it was in S. C. and that
he had command of all troops in that department and Foster
claims he had ought to have command for some reason that I
do not know. That is the story as we get it at Newbern. He
has gone to Washington, D.C. to see about it. It is about time
for him to be back again, he stopped here on his way and
will probably on his return. The general opinion here is that
we shall be defeated as the expedition has been so long about
it and the Rebels have had a long time to fortify, but we hope
it will be successful as a great deal depends on the result in
regard to our own affairs and foreign powers that was the
stepping stone to all our troubles and I should like to see the
place laid in ashes, it was a great disappointment to the boys
that they were not allowed to go to help reduce the city. We
have pretty good times here, living very comfortable, have
enough to eat and drink, of course we have to buy some
things such as butter and milk and all other extras. We can
not expect the Government to furnish such things, although it
would be very acceptable. The Gov. furnishes tea, sugar,
coffee, soft bread, potatoes, salt, fish, molasses, saltpork,
beans, salt, fresh beef three times a week and we make it last
for six meals, hard bread three times a week, that is all I can
think of now. Lieut. Cumston has gone on the Expedition as
a Lieut. of the Ambulance Corps. He belonged to it before
they started. I should like to have been with him, it will be a
splendid sight to see the bombarding, although terrible, but
for all that there is something fascinating about a battle and I

always wanted to see a fight such as that will likely be. How is it now, do you have work enough to keep you busy? Camton raised your price any? He had ought to now at the present price of necessities. I hope there are better times coming. Please let me know how you are getting along. Much love to you from your affect. son W.H. Lord

AMBULANCE - *Today an ambulance symbolizes hope – during the American Civil War the hope was to never need transportation in an ambulance – the conveyances were crude wood with two, three or four wheels, none of which provided a smooth ride. The wounded were stuffed in the rough wagons, to be bounced and rolled to medical assistance amidst blood, dirt and worse from previous passengers. Roads or paths were little more than ruts, adding to the challenge of dragging the injured behind the line of fire. If the soldier was strong enough to survive the rocky ambulance ride he would brag of surviving the "avalanche"...the common term for military ambulances.*

HARD BREAD, *also known as hardtack was a small square biscuit consisting of only flour and water. Although it was hard enough to challenge the strongest teeth this rock solid staple of army fare was frequently invaded by crews of hardy weevils. The hard biscuits were often ground to a powder, by smashing them with a rock or a rifle butt, then mixing the mass with pork fat. This concoction could be used as a spread on bread, or as an ingredient in stew or soup.*

No. 32 - Camp Stevenson, Newbern, N.C. – March 5, 1863
Dear Mother, there is another mail to close to night to send you a few scribblings about little or nothing. My health is about where I wrote last. All is quiet here in camp now. The greatest excitement is in regard to our Barracks, an order was had that there are passes for those who should have the cleanest barracks during the days to be inspected by the officer of the day and to be decided by him, the guard detailed from that company for the next day should be excused from duty and have furlolough all day and that the

company having the one most unclean should furnish the guard for the company that had the best thereby making theirs a double guard. There has been considerable rivalry between them to see which should be the best. It commenced day before yesterday. The officer of the day had hard work to decide which should have it, Company A or K, but finally decided in favor of K. Yesterday it was the same but decided to let A have it as we had it the day before. Today Co. A had to furnish double guard (Capt. Spencer Richardson was rather rough on their crack company, to set what was considered at _____ one of the outside ones_____ _____ at over them yesterday if fell upon Co. C another one of the same grade. Today it has not yet been decided but will probably be soon. If you have any chance to send me any prepared cocoa or chocolate I should not object to it but do not make up a box for that. I have nothing particular to write to night so will bid you good night or either evening, with much love to you and all the family including grand mother. I am as ever your most affect. son, WHL

Also enclosed I send my warrant, please keep it for me and iron it out – damping it a little bit will all smooth out.

No. 33 – Camp Stevenson – Newbern, N.C. – March 14, 1863 – 3 O'clock
Dear Mother, yours of Feb. 23, no. 21, & 26th you thought it was 21 but should be no. 22 & March 1st 22, should be 23, I received this noon with great pleasure, have not had a letter since the 22nd of Feb. It seems a long time and we begin to think it had played out. This is the anniversary of taking of Newbern, we were intending to celebrate it but the Rebs thought they would commence it for us. Early this morning before I got up heard heavy cannonading. At first thought it was celebrating by firing salutes at sunrise but they came most too often for that. Sounded more like a celebration. The 92nd NY Reg., around 300 men, have been on the opposite

side of the river a mile or more distant from our camp for nearly two months to keep the Rebs from building breastworks so as to shell the city. There has been several little skirmishes for the last few days driving in our pickets & not amounting to much but this morning they opened upon the 92nd. They sent in a flag of truce three times to see if our folks would surrender, we told them we did not see it, and they might go back and let their shot come, they were prepared for them. Had no more than got there than it came hot & heavy, our men were behind breastwork without cannon & nothing to protect themselves but their muskets. The Rebs had nineteen pieces of artillery and three thousand troops, so said a Lieut. of the 92nd that was in the fight. Our gunboats soon opened upon them and have cleaned them out. We have sent over another regiment, the 85th N.Y. Our gunboat & artillery were on the shore near our camp all the morning but have now ceased, all except the Rebs have retreated as they have not fired since 8 O'clock this morning. All seems quiet now except once in a while our gunboat sends a shot into the wood. The pickets on the Trout Road to Gaston have been driven in a short distance but have sent out more troops, so have stopped them there. It seems to have been a combined attack on the city all around but they can not have it, the Rebs said they would drive at the Gaston House to day at two o'clock but I guess they will not be able to this day or any until peace is declared. The General intended to have had all the troops pass in review this morning, we got ready, dress coat & white gloves, in time and marched down to the corner of the Barracks when we were ordered back and stacked arms around and put our blouse on in readiness to march a short distance but now still remain in camp & so we should for the present. So the review & celebration has been knocked in the head. We have a new flag staff erected here in camp, intending to raise the flag today & that has been postponed. All is quiet on the front at the present. I am glad to hear you have had a sleigh ride and hope you will have more, if not a sleigh ride, a carriage ride. I have not received yours no. 18, and think you have made a mistake in numbering. I did not send any letter by Mr. Evans as he was going upon the Potomac and thought you would get them quicker by mail than by him. Give my love to Mr. Ellis & Mrs. Seaver, Mrs. Wilcox, Walter, Mrs. Wescott & children and all others that may inquire for me. I am in no hurry for my _____ and you need not trouble yourself much to send them. I should be very happy to see you as you would know. The time is now short before I shall be home so cheer up and be happy. It seems a very short time to us. My lungs do not trouble me now at all and I feel more like myself since I have been sick. To night our company & company A were ordered out a mile from here on picket. Co. K went into _____ & Co. A. were deployed out as skirmishers in front. The surgeon sent down word for me to remain in the barracks and not go with them as I would have liked and not remain behind. Sunday morning the Co.s have returned all safe & sound. We are having all sorts of rumors here now but do not give credit to any of them. There has a steamer left for the North this morning but we at the camp did not know it in time to send by it. There will be a steamer sail in a day or two and will get there nearly as soon. Our pickets have just brought in a Rebel prisoner, he came in & gave himself up, he was in the N.C. Artillery and was in the fight on the other side of the river. Have not heard any particulars. We have sent him to Gen. Foster. All is quiet today and the Rebs have retreated, the 44th will not probably be ordered away at this hour now, got four companies away on picket. Le Cain does belong in Boston, his business I have forgot. I do not think it is any of Grandmother's business if you do write to me. The oftener you do so the better. I like it the more they arrive. Yours of the 5th, no. 23 & 24, I received last evening with great pleasure, no matter about the number that is the mistake. I will rectify it so long as I get them. I have not received my blotting paper from Mr. Campbell. I do not understand why. Give my regards to him. They got their dresses for the ball from some negro wenches down town, and some came from the dramatic company that was in town some time ago. There are a great many officers wives down town. It does not make any difference about Parkinson being promoted, as far as work is concerned there is just as much for all to do. I have gone up one step higher but would not give a fig for the difference. I have been on guard twice last Sunday. I was on our camp guard but it is not very hard and we have got very comfortable quarters in the officers' barracks that are away on picket and I was out of doors only a very short time. Tuesday I took six men & a Corporal & went down to the city to guard General Wessels quarters, it was all I had to see about was that the corporal posted the men every two hours, went about the city & enjoyed myself first rate, so have no fears about my going on guard as it is the easiest work I can do. We have got orders to go to Washington, N.C. tonight. In haste, yours WHL

There will not be any marching or camping probably. WHL

General Wessells – *West Point Graduate – in 1862 led the Army of the Potomac and was Brigadier General of Volunteers.*

Skirmisher – *a soldier sent in advance of the main troop as a scout – also a participant in a skirmish*

The original invitation soldier Lord received was mailed to his mother for safe keeping and is herewith reproduced.

Grand Bal Masque,

In the barracks of Cos. D & B, Mass. 44th Regiment, at Newbern, Feb. 23d, 1863, in commemoration of Washington's birth-day.

ORDER OF DANCES.

Floor Managers.

WILLARD HOWARD,   J. R. RICE,   HARRY T. REED.

1	March and Sicilian Circle	Lee's Quickstep
2	Quadrille	Sullivan's Double Quick
3	Les Lancers	Richardson's March
4	Contra	Skittletop Gallop
5	Polka Redowa	Odiorne's Choice
6	Quadrille	Surgeon's Call
7	Polka	Mary Lee's Delight
8	Contra	Stebbin's Reel

INTERMISSION.

Waltz—Varsovienne—Schottische.

9	Quadrille	Ham Fat Man
10	Waltz	Pas de Seul
11	Quadrille	Dismal Swamp Promenade
12	Contra	Our friends at home
13	Polka Quadrille	Long Acre Gallop
14	Quadrille	Dog Out Race
15	Military do.	Newell's March

Sets formed at the sound of the Clarionet.

N. B.   The thanks of this Association are due to the officers of this regiment for their liberal assistance.

No. 42 – New Berne, N.C. - April 28, 1863
Dear Mother, Yours of the 20th No. 31 - I received with pleasure this morning, so sit myself down to scribble a few lines in return. I have not got much news to send. Sent you a letter on the 25th. You may leave off directing your letters to "Camp Stevenson" as we have moved bag and baggage to the city. Don't you wish you lived in a city in a brick house formerly occupied by a Governor and a Merchant now probably in the Rebel Army. I guess the Rebs will find their houses pretty well marked & seared up plastering. Bunks nailed up on the side of their parlors, glass broken, bedsteads & etc. smashed to pieces and thousands of dollars worth of property all gone to thunder. You at home have had no idea of the waste. Just let an army go through West Roxburry and you might get a little insight in the way we *forage*. All is I hope you or I will never see one march through our little town. Have just received our papers, they gave a very good account of the *Washington Seige*. Much better than that thought for, the latest is morning Journal of the 24th from Frank for which I am much obliged. Also some from Mr. Campbell and Dr. Burgess of Dedham. Gen. Foster has ordered "Washington" to be inscribed upon our banners & all regiments there, all the reinforcements included in that order of the 5th RI which ran the blockade on board of the Escort, which was a daring feat but not so much so as General Foster & staff at daylight, a cannon shot went through his bunk which he had left but a few minutes before. If it had struck him would have struck him near the right shoulder & passed through his body coming out near his left leg and no doubt have proved fatal & a great loss for the government could not have met with. Had funeral services over the remains of our much beloved Surgeon Dr. Ware on Sunday morning last. His remains were sent home on board the mail steamer of that day. Oh that is a great loss not only to us but to our country, they say it was caused by over

working himself, and he took cold in taking care of a nigger wench at Washington. I know you must have been greatly worried while we were in "W" and most of us would have had all our pay due us & bounties & five times as much if need be to have sent word home that we were well, as we knew you would get some large stories at first but the news in our latest papers is quite correct. There are rumors that Col. Lee has been ordered to be ready with his Reg. to go on board of transport for home by the 8th of June. Our officers are making out their mustering out papers. Gen. Foster says that the 44th have seen more service than any other reg. in the field (9 mos. Reg.) and we all begin to think so. The big thing, to get commissions & stay at Fort Warren "Home Guard" why don't they come out where they can get a chance at some of the coats of many colors of some of the skedaddlers, pretty way to go to war. Yes I suppose it is all very nice to parade around & show their pretty clothes & presentations swords, why don't they come where there is a chance to get a little blood on their fingers or where they will have to live on hard luck, no chance to get soft bread for many a day, live in shelter tents & etc. I had rather be a private in the rear rank than to be a Lieut. in the Home Guard & say I have served my country at a fort in the Boston Harbor, it is all very nice to play soldier & to know where you are to sleep at night & to know that you can go home every week for a day or two and <u>flirt</u> around with the girls, yes it is all very nice. We hear that there is an order issued from Head Quarters that all nine months men are to leave their arms and equipment at their posts. I hope it is not so, if so hope they will have some in Boston for us when we arrive there, if not, have us discharged at the wharf and go home as we please. Should look more like a flock of sheep than anything else to march without our arms. Did not have many fears of being wounded amidst all the firing, had too much confidence in our bold & skillful Gen. to fear a defeat, we have been in many a scrape with him & have always got through safely. We all believe if he had had a command at Charleston he would have gained a victory, the boys have no confidence in General Hunter. Would you like to take a boarder, say about the middle of next June. I know of a young fellow now in the Army who intends returning about that time and would like to engage a boarding place, would like your North East chamber if he could have it. Have promised him the place, so do not ask who it is as you have seen him before. Oct. is splendid here in the city, trees are leaved out, roses in blossom & all is lovely and all is "hunk". Right pert I reckon. What would you think if I should tell you that I had worn my drawers six or seven weeks, it is a fact, did not have a change with me. Had my undershirt washed & wore my overcoat to keep from taking cold, rather tough I thought, but am all right now and have a good chance to take decent care of ourselves. Since we left Washington the Rebel women, children & men have been put out of the place about a mile out. Took them two or three days to carry off their things into the country. Serves them right. The rebs wanted to take "W" because it is the county seat & they can not get any conscripts out of that county because they are obliged to hold their meetings in W & they would get a great many there. Gen. Hill expected to get at least seven thousand conscripts in that county but he could not, come on the Mass. Boys or our Big Boy Foster so cool in all the fight. There has an expedition started out from here about three thousand men (43rd & 45th have gone). Write as often as you can and I will do the same. Much love to you, family & friends from your most affectionate son. With a true God Bless. W. H. Lord PS. Why don't father, Frank, George or some of those fellows write, if they want some papers. I will send them some as I have got where there is plenty. Please send me a box if you have not. Send me nine or ten cans of condensed milk, but if you have sent one no matter about the milk.

Forage – soldiers on both sides plundered the civilian countryside for supplies, taking what they needed...food, game, farm animals, etc.

Fort Warren – located on George's Island in the Boston Harbor was a Civil War prison and harbor defense. Building began on the structure in 1833 and took 30 years to construct. Solders in the field often resented those stationed "behind the bullet line".

Banner – or company flag – the banners were often inscribed with battles in which the unit fought

Skedaddlers – a derogatory term for a soldier who ran from battle - also used about those who tried to resist the draft

General Foster – West Point graduate – military governor of New Berne & vicinity – trained as an engineer – died 1874

General Hunter – Tried to capture Charleston but was defeated at Secessionville – criticized for retreating at Lynchburg – raised the first all black South Carolina regiment of soldiers – resigned from the military in 186. Hunter was known as "Black Dave" for his efforts in organizing the black troops.

#43 – New Berne, N.C. May 5, 1863
Dear Mother, mail came in last night but there was nary a letter for me, was some what disappointed in not receiving one but am cheered up by the prospect of getting one soon as a steamer was to leave the next day after the one that came last night. I understand that the same steamer returns this PM. We are now on PG Guard so there is not much of anything exciting going on as you might imagine. There has quite a number of troops gone up to Plymouth, also to Washington. Those at P are in command of Acting Major Gen. Wessel (now Brigader) and I think also Washington troops, we think he is going to clean the rebs out in the vicinity and hope it is so. Our two companies have come down from picket which will make it lighter work for us all. Have received a pkg. of blotting paper from Frank which I am very much obliged. The weather here is very warm and quite uncomfortable; the consequence is that we do not feel much like doing anything. The water here in the city is very poor, clean enough but has a very unpleasant taste making us

very thirsty all the time, but we have one consolation & that is we have only five weeks more and then we all shall be where we can take a drink of pure fresh well water. I suppose the trees and flowers are all leaved out and blossomed at home, all is lovely & the goose hangs high. I have not got much news to write so will now close hoping to get a letter by the next mail from you.

With much love to you and all at home. I remain as ever your most affectionate son. Wm. H. Lord

Goose hangs high – Civil War song – *a repeated refrain was "...everything is lovely, and the goose hangs high". Two possible meanings of the phrase were said to be: The goose was flying (or hanging) high in the sky or the smoked & preserved goose was hanging high and safe from predators in the homestead rafters.*

Was payed off last Saturday four months pay which was quite acceptable. I shall send a box home a few days before I leave New Berne send it to Frank but I do not want it opened until I arrive, he can send it out home but need not open it unless I put these two letters upon it "**A K**", then not until it is home, not that there will be anything in it I am afraid of having you all see but I wish to open it myself, will send by Adam's Express & have it sent to Frank's store. Have had an offer of a commission in the 20th Mass. Vol. also in another reg. but have refused them all. Yours, WHL

No. 44 – New Berne, N.C. May 6, 1863
Ever Dear Mother, Yours of May 1st no. 32 I received last evening just before Taps and very happy was I to receive yours also some from my dear sisters. I have just returned from the rail Depot there was quite a number of families went out on the cars under a flag of truce, outside of the lines by order from Head Quarters from Washington, DC. There has quite a number of families remained that will probably

go out soon. There was a great wailing and gnashing of teeth, crying & there is quite a number of lovely females among them and it seemed more like being in Boston going out on a picnic that it did of turning families out of their homes. The principal excitement of the day is the marriage of Corporal Lawrence of the 44th to a young secesh girl. She was educated in New York and has been here but a few months. There is considerable fun made about it here, her parents & family went out with the Rebs this morning she has remained with her little "Dear Corporal" and will probably go home with the 44th. Some of our cavalry captured some Reb Cavalry, fifteen or twenty. I do not know how or where it was done. I have not yet had any lice upon me, you can tell George I am not in the habit of raising such animals, suppose he must have a fine stock of them ere this, hope he will feed them well. Give my love to him not forgetting Mary, should like to see her first rate. How is it, has Mr. Wason got any good saddle or carriage horses, do not let him know I asked, but really I should like to know. I am sorry and was very much surprised to hear of the death of Mr. Jordon, it must be a great loss to the girls. Give my love to Longs when you see them, also my Grandmother, Mrs. Westcott, Wilcox, and all that may inquire that you think I care anything for. The letter from the girls I will try and answer by this mail if I can. From your most affectionate son, With a True God Bless, Wm. Henry Lord

Lice – also known in the camps as grayback infestations – the creatures were a constant and annoying problem. Soldiers often spent free time boiling their clothes to get rid of the beasts and plucking the bugs from each others hair.
Secesh - a secessionist…supporter of the rebellion

NEWS REPORT – *N.Y. Times* – Sept. 1864 – as reported in the *Union News*

"A Hopeless Malady – All the great Generals whom Jeff Davis sends to command his chief army in the south west seem to be quickly attacked by some mysterious malady whose chief symptom is the appetite for moving backward. Sidney Johnson was first seized by this disease, and after it had driven him across the entire State of Tennessee he communicated the infection to Beauregard. Beauregard gave it to Bragg who had a shocking attack. Bragg left it as a legacy to Jo Johnston whom it assailed furiously. Jo Johnston gave it to Hood who by suddenly staggering back from Atlanta shows that his case has had a bad beginning. Hood swore but a fortnight ago that he would never retreat, that he would stand his ground in spite of fate, or die as in other days Kirby was wont to give up the ghost. But what was the use of his attempting to resist the power of a malady he inherited through four generations of rebel predecessors? We expect to see his affliction take on yet more violent manifestations before long."

Vicksburg – 1864

Brother James, now I set me down with hast to write a few lines to you. It is now 7 o'clock and we are all in a very uneasy humor. We have marching orders to be ready to march at any time and we have all kinds of orders some say one thing and some another. Now I will have to stop before I finish this for our orderly Sergant has just been to my tent door and sed that we must be ready in five minutes to fall in line to march to train to escort the 7 Wisconsin Regement thru town to the base as they have Enlisted over and are veterans they are going home to recrute, when we start from here we will not no whare we will land but the general opinion of all of the officers is that we are going with the expedition of ten thousand up the Red River that is in Louisiana it empties into the Mississippi near Fort Henderson. If this be our disteney we will probably have some fiting (fighting) to do. The Rebles have one gun boat up the river and they also have some strong forts that we no of and then I will probably have a chance to see the city of New Orleans which I would very much like to see. Major General Shurman has returned from his expedertion out in the state of Mississippi he says that he had accomplished all that he intended when he started. They went across the Tombigbey River and they captured five gun boats on the Tombigby River. They burnt everything as they went and lived up to the country and had several squirmishes with the Rebles and whiped them every time. They say that were on the experdission with them that it was the worst experdission that they were ever on. They went 400 miles and all of the way they had squirmishing all around them both in the front and rear and also on both sides. They took a good many Prisners and they lost a good many men in the operation. Now James, I am in exlint (excellent) health and feal as tho old man says Bulley! Now I will have to close thinking that we will be called up in the nite and move. If I get a chance I will get my miniature taken and sent home before long and I would like to have you send yours to me and I want you to tell mother to get hers taken and send it to me. I have not herd from thare in some time now and I want you to write to me soon with out fail. Do give my respects to all and mother and George and also tell aunt Susanna to write me forth with. Thare has another report come to the Regment now stating that our regment is a going to stay here and do all of the picket duty so I will not be surtan (certain) wether we will go or not on this experdission. If we do I will manage to write all of the news when in the field.

Andrew

PROTEST!

As the war among Americans progressed death reached into the homes of nearly every family on both sides of the conflict. More and more men were needed to fill the ranks...the answer was conscription. It became a very unpopular word.

The following drawing, published in "Harpers Weekly", expressed the sentiments of people agitating for a peaceful settlement of the conflict. The next letter describes a young man who fled to Canada in order to escape the draft....but snuck home to visit his family.

August 1864 – Stamford - To Mrs. Peter Burgher
Dear Madam, By request of your husband I write you. On the
second day of August Peter left Owens plase with the entintion of
going home and told me if you or his brother wrote him to answer
the letter and tell you off him. Peter was an excellent hand on the
farm and I was sorry to part with him. But he got most terrible
home sic and made up his mind to make you a visit even at all the
hazards, thinking he would do so in safety. And if <u>ABE</u> should get
him he would not keep him long perhaps on account of the
lameness in his hip. If times seem dangerous he intends to work
away as usual in some by plase and dodge the Lincoln spies. Peter
does this thing with the best intention. He wanted to be nearer his
family and command higher wages in order that he might be of
service and help you to get along during this terrible war. This is
about all I can say. I hope he got home in safety for your sake. His
brother wrote Peter the third of August advising him to stay in
Canada by all means if he could be safe. Tell John & Mr. Burgher
Esq. we got the letter and that hay is worth 15 dollars per ton. Dry
goods are ranging higher than usual. Calico for ladies dresses is
worth from 15 to 25 cents per yard. Cotton shirting ranges from 20
to 30 a yard and so on. The war effects prices in Canada as much
or at the same rate per cent as it does yours. The only difference is
the percentage on the money. Tell Mr. Burgher that Duke Bell got
something like seven dollars of Peter. PS – I should like to have
your answer this note that I may know if Peter is safe and sound.
Yours Truly,
Ralph Kuber

This notice was posted in the state of New Jersey – announcing the call for 300,000 additional drafted men....

STATE OF NEW JERSEY,
EXECUTIVE DEPARTMENT,
Trenton, June 8th, 1864.

CIRCULAR.

It has been officially intimated that a call will soon be made for 300,000 additional men to serve for three years or during the war. I am informed that, in anticipation of this call, the enrollment lists of the several sub-districts are now being revised.

In many districts the former enrollment was imperfect, and injustice was done the people in the assignment of quotas upon such incorrect lists. In most instances errors were brought to the notice of the State authorities too late to procure the proper correction.

It is important that the municipal authorities of the several cities and townships should inspect the new enrollment before it is returned, and have all inaccuracies corrected.

The names of non-residents, aliens, persons deceased, those under or over the required ages, those exempt by reason of physical disability, and those now in the Army and Navy, should be erased from the lists.

JOEL PARKER.

In 1863 it was still possible for a man with cash to **"purchase** *his way out of the responsibility of serving in the military.* **This certificate** *shows that Mr. Robert Smith paid three hundred dollars to be discharged from the obligation.*

The following are love letters from a young soldier, Harley Pelton, to his wife...Mary.

68 NY VV Cleveland Tennissee
Oct. 17th, 1864
Dear Mary I hardly know what to say to you but keep up good courage and take care of your health it is hard to part but the hope of return takes the sting from adieu, it is only for one year, if we can only live and I come back it will be happyness enough to account for some of it, I shall get 16 dollars a month and one hundred dollars Bounty, I have to report at 5 oclock so I have but a few minutes to write we shall leave here this week so I cannot tell when I can write to you again but it will be as soon as I get where I can , but wherever I go your image shall be with me you are my life, my hope all I hold dear on earth and all I have to live for, I will not forsake my god but I will worship you next to him, yours until death.
Harley Pelton to Mary Pelton

Harts Island Sunday October 23 rd, 1864
Dear Mary
I sit me down to write once more to you, my health is good so far, but we are all slaves here, there is no one allowed to vote unless he votes for old Abe, I would rather be in front than here, I do not know how long we shall stay here, we may stay a month and we may not stay two days, but do not grieve or expose your health for I shall be true to you and come back to you as soon as I can get an honorable discharge, and I shal not have to stay over a year. I think I want you to write to me and let me know what they have done at town meeting and concerning all business that you think necessary. I can not get much chance to visit so you must not think hard if I don't write much. I am siting by the side of Joseph Lewis of Parksville he is here. It will be a long year if I have to stay away from you so long, but we

81

may as well put up it the best we can. Take good care of your health and get along as well as you can you need not try to pay any debts only Milton ten Dollars and he has got a ten Dollar order on Bridges that gave to him and a fifteen Dollar note on Lorenzo Cisco that I let him have, other ways I want you to keep all the money you get to help your self with, tell others that want me to write that they will have to wate until I get a better chance to write than I can get here for when I get a chance to write I shal write to you. I want to write to the rest of my folks and yours, but I can not yet for we are kept on duty most of the time. I want you to write as soon as you receive this so I can get it soon as I can, but if I leave the Island before I get it I will write to you as soon as I can, remember that every day counts one and a year will role around after a while and happy will be the day if we can ever meet again both alive and well and I hope and trust we shall so I remain your true and faithful husband Mary Pelton ,
Harley Pelton
Direct to Company - H - Harts Island
New York Harbor, New York

Bridgeport Allabamma,
November 10th 1864
Dear Mary I have at last arrived at the Rejiment to which I was assigned, William Bowland, Willis Cook, Lewis Fuller, Billy Fuller and myself are all together, but we are in a german Rejiment they use us first rate here, we only got here to day it is an old Rejiment that has been all cut to pieces, it is now stationed here to guard the Railroad between Nashville and Atlanta so the prospects is that we shal not see much fightin, I never suffered more hardships in the same time than I did in getting here, it rained every day for 10 days and good share of the time we had to lay on the ground with the mud over shoe at that, but I have stood it good so far and have had no trouble with anyone, I have a good many things to tell you when I come home that I cannot find room

82

for here concerning way we were used before we got here, all the trouble I see now is on your account I am in such a hurry to hear from you that I can hardly wate until I get a letter, so please sit down and write me a good long letter tell me everything you can think. Tell me if aunt Amy is with you and how you get along you must do your own planning just as you think best until I get back, I shall get 16 Dollars per month and 100 dollars government bounty when the year is up, keep up good courage Mary and take good care of your health I think we have if there is anything that you want my advice upon you can let me know and I will write it back, tell me how you have got along with your work and what was done at town meeting, what you have done with the sheep and so forth, and more than all how is your health and tell me truly for I feel anxious to hear, you must think strange of this scribbling for I sit cramped up in my tent writing on a piece of board about three inches wide, so good night Dear Mary from your true and faithful Husband Wm H Pelton

Direct your letters to Wm H Pelton Company B 68th Regt, NY Vol., BridgePort Allabamma
I will write to Milton as soon as I get another chance so good Night and may God bless you and keep you safe HP

As soon as we draw any pay I will send you some money

Bridgeport November 27th, 1864
Dear Mary, again I seat myself to send my love to you, and let you know that I am yet well and hearty and god knows how anxious I am to hear that this finds you the same, I looked some for a letter from you last night but it did not come but I shal look for one this week sure we had two cold Nights last week the ground frosen about two inches deep but it is warm weather again now, you must take all the comfort you can and be as contented as you can for we are having easy times here now, the only thing that worres me is

thinking of your staying there without me to care for you but I hope it may all turn out well yet. Oh if we only have our health and I come back next fall we will know how to prize each others society with thankful hearts to god for restoring us again to each other, so let us trust in his goodness and I do not think that that he will forsake us but bring us back to love and Peace again, you must keep up good courage Mary two months has almost passed already, I have the good will of all the men and officers so far, if any one received any favors it is generally Wm Pelton to be the favored one, if any hard job is to be done they send the subs and tell me to never mind and get milk of the farmers when I want it, there some things I would like you to send me and I think you will be glad to send them to me. I want you if it is not to much trouble to send me some things in a box, have Milton fix a box that will hold about fifty lbs of stuff, tell him to nail hoops around the ends the same as a dry goods box then get a couple of tea canisters if you can think of nothing better and pack them full of pickled cabage and sement the tops so they cannot leak and put them in the box then get a Pail or something that will hold about four quarts and pack it full of smoked eels and set that in the box also, then pack the box with onions and sent it to me, get Milton to take it to the flat and pay the freight on it, Burr Wilson will know how to direct and send it, he can send it to the Railroad by O.L. Sherwood thence by Adams Express, I will pay all the trouble as soon as I can if Milton will see to it for you, there is some of the boys here that wants me to get them, they are good fellows and willing to pay their share. One thing more that I forgot that is two or three pounds of fine salt for this is a very scarce article with us, put in a ball of yarn and Darning needle to darn my socks. I think it will be a pleasure to you to send it to me and it certainly would be a pleasure to me to receive it from you, tell me if you have got your flannel yet, I must now close by biding you good Night and may god bless and care for you and keep you safe until I return to you again, so I remain

your true and faithful Husband Harley Pelton. Direct the box
to the same as the letters

*SMOKED EELS - a very popular and plentiful food in early
America. Rivers were full of the snakelike fish and frequent
harvests of the creature were common. Stone weirs were
constructed in rivers to divert migrating ells toward shore
and more convenient capture.*

Bridgport, Jan 15th, 1865
Dear Mary I once more take my pen in hand to let you know
I am getting along, well soon after I wrote you last we were
ordered out to join Shermans forces to drive Hood from
Nashville, well we was on the march for over a month. I saw
some fighting but not much. We had a hard time although it
rained over half of the time we had to march through mud
half knee deep and ford streems nearly to our waist, over half
of the men gave out and had to be left behind, I kept up good
and we are back to our old camp again thank god, where I
can write to you again. I expect you have thought me dead
before this time but I have turned up again all right so far we
expect to stay here to guard the railroad the rest of our year
but we cannot tell we may be ordered out again. I have to go
on guard every third day and stay on twenty four hours and
stand on post two hours and off four I am on guard to day so
I cannot write much, but when we get our shanty built I shal
write longer letters and more of them, I wrote you once what
I wanted you to send in a box but I expect you did not get it,
I will let you no in my next what I want. We can get paper
and stamps here now, I received those of yours, they came
verry good but I never received a letter from you until we got
back and the latest one I got was Dec. 2, this letter is just to
let you know that I am alive and well and where I
am. I will write more particulars in my next. I am glad to
hear that you get along so well and I don't want you to worry
if there is times that you don't get letters for the road may be

cut or I may be where I cannot wirte but you know I will doo
my best to let my Mary how and where I am for my thoughts
are all with you, I must close now for it is about time to fall
in for second relief from your faithful husband Harley Pelton

Bridgeport Feb. 12th 1865
Dear Mary another week has passed away and I am still alive
and well and every week shortens so much the space of time
that seems to go by with such a dead weight between us, I do
not know but I am wicked for wanting the time to pass away
so fast but it is a weekness I cannot help for would be willing
the remainder of the year to pass away as quickly as my
thoughts could turn to you if it could only bring me back to
you in the same time, Mary if we had not lived so happy
together it mite not seem so cruel to be separated, you have
often told me that we took to much comfert to have it last
long, and I do not know but you was right, still I hope to
have the good fourtune to return again to you and the
happyness I have left, I shal keep up good courage as long as
I can hear from you and know that you are well and faring
well, and I want you to keep up good courage and remember
that god will watch over us as well in one place as another, if
it is according to his will that we shal meet again to live and
enjoy each others society all the Niggor wars and relations in
the world cannot prevent it, but if it is not then we must
school our hearts to bear his chastening rod as best we can,
Mary I will never think my living to poor or my work too
hard again if I can only be permitted to pass the remaining
days with my own true hearted Mary, I have just received a
letter from you dated Dec, 8, No.4, in which Aunt Amy
wanted to know how I get my washing done, and the answer
is I have to do it myself, Aunt Amy I know you wish in your
heart that you could do it for me but that is out of the
question, but I am just as thankful for the wish as tho you
could do the kindles but more than all else that I have to
thank you for is for your care of Mary and I want you to

remember that one favour shown her is the same as ten to me, and I think if the prayers of a poor soldier can avail any thing that you will both have more than an ordinary share of comfort yet, I have not much news to write this time only the rejiment went out on another raid the other day they got back yesterday, they captured 17 gurrillas and as many horses, I did not go out this time, I would like to write a longer letter but I have not time but oh Mary remember the comfort we have taken in each others society and take good care of your health that you may live to enjoy many more happy days with me if I have the good luck to come back to you and my little cottage home, Good Night Dearest Mary, Harley Pelton

BridgePort Alabama March 2th, 1865
Dear Mary, it is with the greatest pleasure that I take my pen to inform you that I received your box yesterday and it gladdens three hearts I can tell you for by some neglect of the quarter-master we had not got any rations in two days accept a pint of weak coffee twice a day and a pint of soop once a day and verry poor at that with a piece of poor beef so you may know how opportunely it came, I was at work on the fort when I heard that my box had come to the quarter masters so I droped my tools and started, and got it, I will tell you now if I have not before that my friend Charles E. Smith is an officer and stays at head quarters but he is the same true friend to me that he always has been, I think I spoke of another friend of mine by the name of Fredrick Dart from Connecticut, we stay in our shanty yet, its 8 x 12 feet with a fire place to cook by, and he and I live like brothers or like Father and son for he is only 16 years old but he is a good boy and has had a rather hard time of it in the world so far, he talks as though he should come home with me when our time is out and get a place to work some where near me if he can, well I sent for Smith when I got my box and I divided between us three all only what you told me I must not but I gave them a taste of all and they was pleased with it I can tell

you, they send their best respects, and all the good wishes
they can think of to you, the needle case I gave to Smith I
made a mistake in reading the paper in mine I thought you
sent it for me to give to a friend I mentioned, and I told him
so, land he was pleased enough with it for we only had one
needle an about 6 threads between us, and he is asked me if I
was willing he should answer it himself instead of sending
his thanks through my letters he said would like to if I
thought you would not take any offence, I told him I did not
think you would and I certainly should not, so if he does you
must not be offended for I have been with him long enough
to know that he is not a man that would wish to insult any
woman, for he has got a wife in New York that he thinks his
eyes of, he has promised that he and her will come up in the
country and make you and me a visit when our time is out,
our time will all be out at once but I think they will wait until
the next summer and then I think they will come for his wife
writes in about every letter she is making more reconing on
coming than any other place he could of promised her to go,
he has wrote so much to her about me that she wants us to
send our likeness together so when we get our pay we are
going to have them taken together and send to her and you,
he is out of money now as well as the rest of us and he will
not write home for any, but his wife writes to him that she
will send him all the money he wants but he keeps waiting
for the paymaster to come and pay us off, well when I came
to read the paper to day I found that Aunt Amy had sent the
Nedle book and I had told him wrong, so I guess I will let it
go so now it will not make much diference any way but he
was verry pleased with what I got, everything came good and
was in good order, tell Milton, Hannah, Frances and Barney
that I am thankful to them for what they sent me for it is a
good treat to me and I am very thankful to you and Aunt
Amy for taking so much pains for me, you can not tell how
much good it has done me to have some things from home, it
has nourished my mind as well as body, it was like Noahs

dove returning to the ark with the olive branch after its long absence, tell Milton I sent him a letter about a month ago and I have not received an answer yet, I would like to know if he got it, the order has come from Sherman now for us to stay here and hold this Post this summer so if it is not countermanded we shall likely stay here until our time is out, for my part I hope we shal stay where we are, well I will try and send you some of my officers names they are all german but the Colonel and he is a Prussian.

Colonel Felix Prince-Salem Salem
Lieut, Col. A. Von Stienhausen
Major Arnold Krimmer
Adjt. Carl Riese
Capt. Co B, Alfred Von der Groeben
1st Lieutenant, Adolph Joseph
1st Sergeant David Glauber

You may think that I am hasty in forming a friendship with C. E. Smith but he has proved himself a friend to me so far in every respect when I was sick and had nothing that I could eat, and no money to get anything with he went and got me some tea and bread and butter and milk and sugar and some fresh fish and fetched it to me, and I tell you it done me good, then he took a five dollar bill out and handed me, I told him I did not want to take it for we mite be separated and I would never have the chance to pay him again, he told me that he should have the pleasure of knowing that he had helpcd a friend and that wall all the pay he wanted, I can not help but think that he is a friend to me, we have went through some hard scenes together and where either of us would of fainted by the way if it had not been for the other to cheer him on, Well Mary I am glad to hear that your health is no worse than when I left you and I will tell you the truth as to mine it has never been better to my knowledge, I am perfectly well for all I know to the contrary, and tuff as a Mule if I had not been I could not went through all I have and come out alive, if I could get enough to eat I would not grumble but it may be all the better for my health if I can only have my health as good until my time is out how thankful I shal be, good night Dearest Mary your true and faithful husband Harley Pelton

The picture is of an authentic home made sewing kit carried by a Union soldier during the war years.

No. 1 Sunday March 12, 1865 - Bridge Port Alabama
Dear Mary I received your kind letter yesterday Mailed Feb.
27, and I am so thankful to hear that you keep your health
and get along so well, I hope you will keep up good courage
and have your health good until I get back 7 more months
and I will be free again if I live to see that time which I am in
hopes I shal, I do not have so much duty to do as I did I am
at work on the forts yet, I have to work 8 hours a day but I
take it verry easy, they talk now of setting me to making axe
handles for the Rejiment if they do I shal be my own boss
and it will be easier yet for me, I shal have a man to help get
out the timber ready to finish off. I do not have any more
guard duty to do as it is but I intend to get as easy a place as I
can while I stay, you wanted to know if I had any pay yet,
well I have not but I get along verry well now, I have got
friends enough here that will help me to anything I ask, some
of them are officers to, we have put in a new Cook in our
company, we found out that our cook was robing us of our
rations so we turned him out and put in a new one, so we fare
a little better on that account, I got a letter from Lester
Stewart yesterday and answered it, it was the first I have
written to Bills boys, I got a letter from you yesterday dated
Feb. 2 and one from Milton dated about the same time, the
reason of the Mail being delayed so long was on account of
an awful flood in the rivers here it swept away some of the
Railroad bridges but it has got to going again, yesterday
there was a rebel Captain of Cavelry and his whole Company
over 60 in number with all their horses guns revolvers and all
other equipment came into our camp and gave themselves up
as Prisners, well I received the box you sent and I sent you a
letter rite back stating all the particulars, please let me know
if you received that letter, my box was all right and
everything nice and I have some of the fruit and sugar yet, I
can manage now to get what I need in the way of Tobacco
and grub, as for clothing there is no lack of that so don't risk
sending any more boxes, I sent a letter yesterday to Pa, I

hope they will get it, Mary let us number our letters I will commence with this so when you receive this commence with No. 1, number them on back of the paper like this is, then when you send a letter keep the number of it on a paper by its self and when you receive one from me take down the number by its self also then we will know how many letters we loose, Mary I will send you my likeness as soon as I can get Paid, it costs a good deal to get them taken here, but when we get our pay I intend to send you all three of our likenesses, my own and Smiths and Darts so you can see how my tent mates look.

Bridgeport, *Alabama is located in the Tennessee Valley in the Appalachian Mountains. During the Civil War ten redoubts were constructed in 1863 by Confederate troops using slave labor for the defense of Bridgeport. The Union captured Bridgeport late in 1863.*

***US Christian Commission**– aid society for Union armed forces
created in NYC in 1861 by the YMCA – provided many services
including writing materials, nurses, Bibles, free food and coffee.
The photos show a typical CC Camp and stationery
letterhead.*

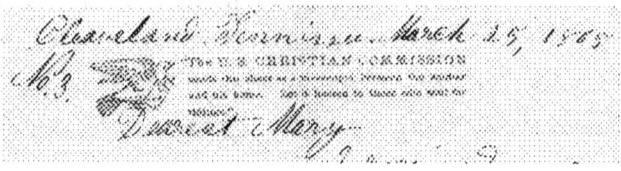

Cleveland Tennisee, March 25, 1865, No. 3

Dearest Mary, I received your kind letter of the 12 yesterday and I was rejoiced to hear that you are still getting along so well, we have mooved as you see to this place we are expecting to stay here some length of time. It may be 2 or 3 weeks and it may be all summer I cant tell, it is a nice and healthy place here, the Peach trees are in full bloom and have been for several days, I have just got me another shanty completed and am sitting in it and writing to you, my health still remains good, you asked me if my officers were good to me, I answer yes, they favour me in everything they can and that is everything I ask and more too and if they want anything made nice or any little piece of work done to suit them and look nice they think there is no one can do it but Pelton and if I don't help them more than one hour in a day it will clear me from all other duty for 24 hours, there has none of the officers that ever spoke a cross word to me yet but they are verry strict with the most of the boys. There is one poor fellow now stands tied to a tree with his hands behind him to remain so for four hours. He is a good fellow too and a good friend to me, I have just been out talking with him and gave him a chew of tobacco that is all I can do for him for they keep a guard over him. You said the bantys had began to lay. I want you to set them both and raise me all the chickens you can, if they are not too much trouble. Well Mary take good care of your health and aunt Amy to, I want you both to take good care of your selves and keep your health and I shal endever to do the same. I shal soon bee on my last half year. I wish it was the last half day of my time of service but it will come round after a while then I will hurry home to my own true hearted Mary. Again with the assurance that her heart has not grown cold in my absence for I know as long as you live your heart will still beet warm and true for me. Good night Dearest Mary from your true and faithful husband, Harley Pelton

No 4 – Cleveland Tennissee April 1, 1865
Dear Mary I have just received your letter of March 19 and
set me down to answer it, Mary you cannot know how much
your letters cheer me, judge if you was as far away from
your home and in a strange land and had not been inside of a
house in six months whether you would not be still more
anxious to get a letter from home, then than you can be now,
it is true I have got good friends here and am favored more
than any other private soldier in the rejiment but war in an
enemies country is not peace at home, everything here goes
by the military rule, we can see all the implements of war
every day but I cannot see any thing that looks anything like
peace, we have just got into camp again after another raid,
there is a gang of about 3 or 4 hundred gurrillas here in east
Tennissee we have been after them but they have all got
horses so we did not get one of them, I think likely we shall
have to hunt bush wackers all summer but if we move our
camp again I shal let you know, I have sent you the address
to this place once but perhaps you did not get it, I will send it
again, keep good courage Mary, my time is most half
expired and I am in good health yet and hope I may remain
so, when I am in camp now I have it very easy although I am
busy nearly all the time at some light and easy work which I
would soon do as lay still, I have been helping the officers
fix their shanties ever since I got mine done, only when we
were on the raid, tomorrow I am going to help Lieutenant
Josephs fix a fence and make a little garden for him back
side of his tent, I have new tent mate now he bought Dart out
so he could tent with me, Dart was out of money and wanted
some verry bad so he sold out and went in with Bill Rowland
my tent mates name is Henry Legacy, he is a Frenchman 22
years old and just about my size but he can talk English as
well as I can, he is a good lively fellow and we get along first
rate so far, as to that I do not have any trouble with any one
here , but Mary there can be no other friend like you if it was
not for your kind loving letters I could not stay so contented

as I do, they fill me with hope and cheer me in all my lonely hours for you know I can not help but be lonely when parted from the best and dearest friend I can ever have in this world, although there may be thousands around me still I cannot help but feel lonely when you are not with me, good night Dearest here is your kiss from your ever faithful husband To Mary Pelton, Harley Pelton

Direct to Wm. H. Pelton CO B

Cleveland – April 30th 1865

Dearest Mary,

Again I resume my pen to inform you that I am stil at Cleveland and my health is full as good as when I left home, I have got to inform you that I have given up all hopes of being discharged until my time is out, we expect to leave here within a week but I do not know our destination they say we are to take command of some of the Block Houses along the Railroad but where I do not know, so we shal have to make up our minds to wait with patience until next fall, but don't get discouraged Dear Mary there is only five months and six days that they can keep me before I can demand my discharge and return to my Mary again who is so patiently waiting for me, I know you will be disappointed when you hear this but it cannot grieve you worse than it does me for I did have hopes of being with you again by the fourth of July, but cheer up Mary I shal take as good care of my health as I can and I want you to be sure and do the same, it is not likely that we shal have any more fighting to do, hold on a minute the whole Regiment is in an uproar I will just step out and see what is the matter, well here it is, there has a Dispatch just arrived from Secretary Stanton that there is to be 150,000 men mustered out of the service between now and the first of July but whether it will include this regiment or not I can not tell but I think not, so now Dear Mary manage your business as you think best, I am

sorry that I cannot be there to take the care on myself but I
cannot yet a while, well to day is muster day again, we are
mustered every two months and get no pay at all and there is
no prospects of our getting payed until our time is out then
we will be likely to get it all at once it may be better for us, I
can not think of any more News to write, tell Aunt Amy she
must not be discouraged for I will be home as soon as I can
and try and recommence her for her trouble and kindness.
Now do not let your spirits go down for I hope to see better
times for all of us before a great while longer, it is from
Grants Army that those men are to be discharged and we are
to stay our time out but I thank god that is not only a little
over five months and it will roll around after a while, the
time seems long but it can not last always and if we can only
be blessed with good health and patience to wait for that day
that brings me home again to you it will be the happiest day
that I have ever sen, so good Night dearest Mary from your
own Harley P. Cleveland Tenn, or else where.
Please keep this mans address, Mr. Albert G. Price,
Cleveland, Bradley County, Tennissee he wants me to write
to him as soon as I get home, H. Pelton

No. 9 – Dalton, Georgia – May 7th 1865
Dearest Mary I once more resume my seat to write to you,
we are now on the railroad between Dalton and Atlanta,
there are a considerable force of Lees and Jacksons men in
front of us commanded by General Warford, there is some
talk of their surrendering and I think they will for they
cannot fight their way much past here, I expect we shal go on
through this state by the way of Atlanta, we cannot go any
further by rail for the road is destroyed from here. so we shal
have to march it if we go, so you need not write again until
you get another letter from me for I should not get it if you
did, and I do not expect to have a chance to send another
until we arrive at some station else where, I cannot tell
anything about how long that may be, you spoke of sending

me money but I don't want you to do it for I should not stand
a half a chance to get it, Don't get discouraged Dear Mary
they cannot keep me only five months more then if the Lord
sees fit to spare us we may look forward to a happy reunion,
you may think it strange that we are not to be discharged as
soon as any but we belong to a separate reserve for the
purpose of protecting the Railroads from the Gurrilla bands
which still continue to infest the country, so you need not
look for me home until my time is expired, but keep up good
courage Dear Mary autumn will come again after a while
then I hope to return once more to you and live the rest of
my life in quiet with the one I love so truly and the one I
know to be the best and truest friend I have on earth and
whose love I know will never fail me, I shal let you know
my where abouts as soon as I have an opportunity, so don't
be uneasy about me the most to be feered here now is the hot
weather but I am in hopes to stand that pretty good my health
is about the same as when I wrote last, I have received no
letters from Sanesboro yet, and we have received no pay yet
and no prospects of any yet a while, but it will come after a
while, give my respects and thanks to Miltons folks for their
kindness to you, tell Aunt Amy I remember her, give my
respects to all who inquire after me, I now close so good
Night Dear Mary from your true and faithful Husband
Harley Pelton

No. 22, Chatahoocha, Dec. 20, 1865
Dearest Mary,
We have just received orders to move to Savana the relief
has just arrived we shall perhaps start tomorrow morning,
but it will not make any difference with our getting
Discharged we shal be discharged on the 20th so you need
not answer this for it is not likely I would get it, but keep up
good courage if we only live and have our health it will not
be long before we shal meet again, the boys are all well and
anxious to get home, you must excuse me this time for I have

but little time to write, but I am your own true Harley still and when I get home to you I can tell you more than I can write, from your true and faithful Husband Harley Pelton

Bridgeport Jan 30, 1865
Dear Mary this is to let you know that I am yet alive and well we have just returned into camp again after another hard march we got in last Night or this morning rather at about three oclock, there were two hundred of us detailed to go out after gurrillas, we wer gone four days we surprised their camp in the Night but they most all got away, they did not fight more than ten minutes before they jumped on their horses and ran off, they left guns saddles blankets Provisions and some of their clothing, we took two prisoners and one wounded man, I don't know how many was killed for the fighting was all done in the woods and I don't think the ground was examined, we lost one lieutenant shot through the head and captured three of their horses but the next day they mustered all the forces they could and overtook us and attacked our rear and drove them like sheep, I was in with the advance so we formed in line of battle and let our rear pass through the line, we then charged upon the rebs and drove them back, it was warm work for a few moments but it was soon over, three of them fell from their horses and I saw a number of riderless horses, the fight was in a swamp, one horse ran out into the road so we took it along, it was nearly dark so we did not search the ground but made our way for the gun boat to fetch us back to Bridgeport again from which we was distant some 75 miles, strange to say we had no one hurt in the last fight, to day we have been to bury the lieutenant, I made several good shots in the fight, I think I killed three or four big trees if a rifle ball will kill a tree, I made the sap run out of them anyway so I am pretty sure they are wounded, well Mr. C. E. Smith sits beside me writing to his wife so you see there are other good fellows that are away from their loved ones, we have our own fun

here as well as our hardships, oh by the way my friend C has got to be an officer now but we are all the same, I received your letter of Jan 8th, and 10th , I have received 7 from you in all up to this date and oh how glad I was to hear that you was getting along so well you and Aunt Amy, I shal be so thankful if you can have your health and get along good until I get back, and I get back safe and sound, I shal not care then for all the hardships that I have to endure, for I think I am gaining health down here so far and you need not feer but what I will look out for number one as long as there is any chance, you need not mind what C. Willis writes for I believe he worries himself so that he is getting nearly crazy, he does not act like the boy he used to be, not by any means, this is the first chance I have had to write to any one since last Sunday and I cannot tell when I shal get another chance to write but I hope as soon as next Sunday at farthest, so now Dear Mary I must go to bed to dream of you an my hapy home where I hope again to be before another winter comes, so good night dearest Mary from your true and faithful Husband Wm H. Pelton
PS Please remember me to Aunt Amy and all the friends around, the Seargent of the guard has just ordered us to put out our light so I shall have to stop at once, here is your good night kiss, Harley

MISCELLANEOUS LETTERS

August 28, 1863 - Binghamton
Dear Son I send you a letter from Win, I think if we are a going to Nanticock we must do it soon or not go at all for I want to go to Michig. as soon as the first week in Oct. If I go this fall Write soon & let me know what you intend to do about going to those places with me & how soon you will be ready to go if you go at all. We are in usual health.

Henry was so "lucky" as to get a prize in Uncle Sams lottery of $300. which as a loyal and patriotic soldier he handed it over to the provost marshall for the benefit of the government in finishing up this rebellion which according to present appearances will be accomplished before old Abes time expires in being at the helm, in spite of all the copperheads can do to prevent it. Henry has engaged to preach at Factoryville in Alleganey and Livingston counties in this state. He commences the first Sabbath in next month. Yours as ever, Jared

Copperheads – *a person from the North who opposed the war – a southern sympathizer.*

This newspaper notice was printed in 1863

A bounty certificate from 1865.

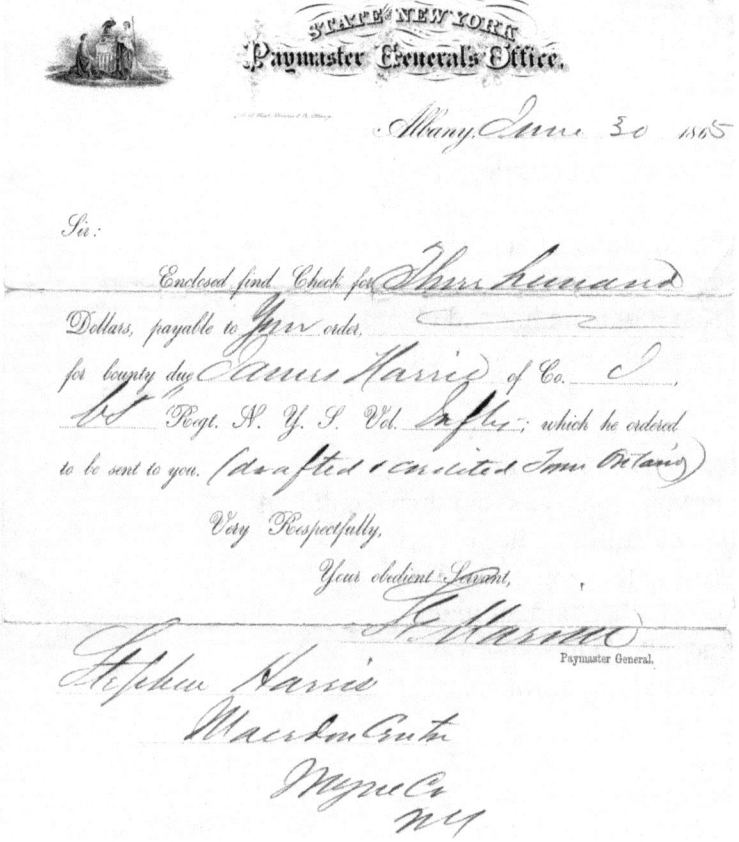

STATE OF NEW YORK
Paymaster General's Office.

Albany, June 30 1865

Sir:

Enclosed find Check for *Three hundred*
Dollars, payable to *your* order,
for bounty due *James Harris* of Co. *I*,
bt Regt. N. Y. S. Vol. *Rifles* ; which he ordered
to be sent to you. *(drafted & enlisted Town Bristol)*

Very Respectfully,

Your obedient Servant,

S. Harris

Paymaster General.

Stephen Harris
Macedon Centre
Wayne Co
N Y

Brothers! Our country Calls us –
Heard ye that startling cry?
Forward by tens of thousands –
Our Union must not die.
Her ruddy sons must rally,
From mountain hill and glen.
Our Country calls for Men!

By every hope of Freedom,
By every hope of life,
For your sons, your children's children
Be ye manful in the strife,
Trust in the God of Battles –
Day shall be born of night,
And out of sin and sorrow
He will bring forth the right.

Bermuda Hundreds - 1864
Dear Friend, I thought I would write you a few lines to inform you that I am well at present & hope these lines find you the same, we have not got our Regt. Yet but expect to join the Regt. Tomorrow or at least I hope we shall for I am sick of being doged around so much. We have been to city 2 days & we did not fare as well as a good farmers dog, could not go out of camp even after water unless we was under guard, have to take a guard all the way & we can't get half enough to eat & what we do get is not fit to eat, if we had not any money with us we would suffer – but the most of us has got money & we get the most of our victuals at the *Sutlers* &

Eating Saloons but I wish I could be home long enough to take a good ride and have something good to eat but I do not think I am homesick for I am not. I feel as gay as a peacock & full of fun – there is some one playing the violin in the camp & it makes me think of home & the party at John S. Is Leroy S. home now & how does he & Ophelia get along, are they going to be married – if they are married before I get back I shall give them a Hail Columbia – well I can't think of any more to write tonight so will write tomorrow – good night with a kiss – Good morning I can't help think where was 12 weeks ago last night & this morning – two weeks ago last night I were with yourself & I was very happy & 2 weeks ago this morning I was home – I am a hurry to get to Petersburg so to see Leroy for I want to see him more than any one else now for it is most 2 years since I have seen him. I am less than 10 miles from him & I don't suppose he knows I am within 500 miles of him. Julia I want you to have your photograph taken & send me one for I want to see you very much. Have Alba send hers to you, don't know how much good it would do me. Have you got my photograph yet? I left one for you – I went to my Brother's & left all names to send to. I can't think of any more so I will close – direct mail to me at 16th Indep. Battery NYV Washington, DC – excuse poor writing & mistakes Phill

Sutlers – *vendors, traveling traders or peddlers, merchants*
Hail Columbia – *The first American national Anthem was "Hail Columbia", composed for George Washington's inauguration as President – sung often by Union soldiers in the Civil War*
Bermuda Hundreds – *A small village in the south east of Virginia on a peninsula between the James and Appomatox rivers. It was founded in 1613. The Union forces were stuck here after a defeat at Drewrys Bluff – in May 1864.*

Feb. 10th 1865
Camp Fort Fisher, N.C.
Dear Friend, I have just rec'd. yours of Jan. & was glad to hear from you. I was very much surprised to hear of Eugene L's death. I can't think what could be the matter with him he was such a healthy little fellow. I think Mr. L. must be most discouraged for I think Della must be dead. I wish I could be there to enjoy some of the Donations that they are having around there this winter & sleighing, it must be very nice, I have not had a sleigh ride in a long time. I am in NC now & the weather is very cold but it will soon be warmer. We left our camp in Va. The 24th of Jan. & got here the 6th of Feb. We come on a steamer & our horses was so crowded that they fell down & there they lay on top of each other struggling for life & we had to work most all night to get them up & 7 of them was dead before we got them up & most all of them was so badly hurt that there was 23 of them dead now. One dies most every day & when we got here we had to swim them about 20 rods to get them to the shore, there is no news of importance to write. There is considerable firing this morning from the Gun Boats we have got a victory here when we got *Fort Fisher*, for there is the greatest lot of artillery that I ever saw – there is one gun in particular that England presented to Jeff Davis – it is mounted on mahogany wood & this captured piece is now the nicest piece of artillery that there is in the whole Union Army. I cant think of any more to write of any importance so I will close hoping to hear from you soon – this from your friend – PS please excuse all mistakes & accept this from your best friend. My respects to Addie.

Donations – *parties held to raise funds and goods for donation to the war effort*

Fort Fisher – Built to guard Wilmington, North Carolina harbor. It was the last major fort to be captured by Union forces during the war...January 1865. Pictured is a photo of the captured cannon discussed is the previous letter.

*Civil War monuments often list the number of **horses** killed along with the total of soldier's dead....in many battles more horses than men lost their lives. This homemade silk wrap for horseshoe nails was lovingly crafted for a soldier in the Union Calvary.*

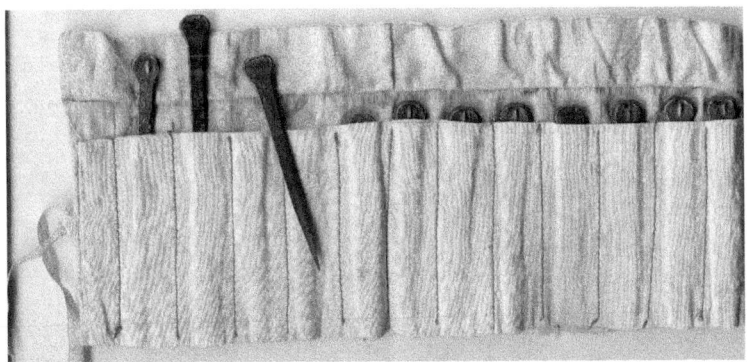

Raleigh, N. C. April 20th 1865, Comp. 16 NY Battery
Dear Friends,
I thought I would write a few lines this evening. I am well at
present & enjoying good Health as ever I did in my life. We
are Encamped about 1 mile from Raleigh, it is a very
pleasant City but the buildings are old & old Fashioned. I
was up to the City this Forenoon & I wish you could have
seen what was going on. There was a General Review of our
troops. Generals Sherman, Sheridan & Terrey was the men
that reviewed us & it was a Splendid sight to see. So many
soldiers marching through the streets. I suppose you must
have heard of our great Victorys of the passed month. Well I
have reason to believe that all Soldiers will be home in less
than 2 months & I hope we may for I dread the hot summer
down here for it is so warm here now that a man is
uncomfortable. Well I cant think of any more to write at
present so I will close please write soon & accept this from
your true friend and excuse fool writing

ABRAHAM LINCOLN

The following letter adds an interesting footnote to history.
If this missive can be believed, perhaps President Abraham
Lincoln did not write the entire Gettysburg Address in a
railroad car....

W. G. Smyser *was a surgeon's assistant during the Civil*
War. This letter was carefully handwritten and preserved
with his entrance and discharge certificates, and a copy of
his family tree.

On July first, second and third 1863 there was fought at the
little town of Gettysburg, Penn., one of the most important
battles of history. Important not for the number of
contestants engaged therein, nor for the terrible loss of life
and suffering there from resulting, but because of the vital
issue involved – the preservation of our nation.

It is not my intention to dwell upon the details of that battle,
but to state briefly one of the resultants of that momentous
struggle viz: the time and place where was written or
completed the grandest, greatest most eloquent speech that
was ever uttered by mortal lips – the address delivered at the
consecration of the National Cemetery at Gettysburg, by him
the Centennial of whose birth we and all other Americans are
this day observing.

Gettysburg is my native place and there my father practiced
law until selected as one of the district judges of the State.
Being required to reside in his district, the then 7th, the
family moved to Norristown, a suburb I may say of
Philadelphia.

Immediately following the battle Judge Wills conceived the
idea of securing a tract of land to be used as a common burial
ground for the dead, then only partially buried over the miles

of territory around Gettysburg. He secured an option on about 17 acres of land on the highest point of Cemetery Hill, the centre of our line of battle of July 2nd and 3rd and overlooking the entire battlefield.

The respective governors responded favorably and immediately appointed commissioners and agreed to urge their legislatures to make appropriations to defray their proportionate share of the expense of carrying out the contemplated work.

Upon the assembling of these state commissioners, Judge Wills was selected as President. The land having been purchased, the eminent landscape gardner William Saunders, was engaged to lay out the grounds. As soon as this was done the bodies were carefully taken up, placed in separate coffins and reinterred in the places assigned them.

It was deemed advisable to consecrate the cemetery with appropriate ceremonies – Oct. 23, 1863 was named as the date and Edward Everett invited to deliver the oration. He accepted the invitation but at his request a postponement of the date was made to November 19th when the ceremonies was held.

Chief among the distinguished men of the nation invited to be present and participate in the exercises was President Lincoln. He with Secretary of State Seward and others reached Gettysburg by special train about six o'clock the evening of November 18th. The President was driven from the station direct to the Wills home. He was shown to his room and in a few moments came down to the parlor where we were all gathered to receive him. After supper we again assembled in the parlor and I can now distinctly see him as he sat in a large arm chair, clasping in each arm one of my then youthful nieces. After probably an hour he asked to be excused saying he would retire to him room as he had some matters to look into and to prepare himself for the morrow when as he understood he would be expected to make a few remarks following Mr. Everetts oration. He then bade us good night and Judge Wills accompanied him to his room. In a few moments the judge came down and going to him office, which was connected with the main hall of his residence, got some paper with pen and ink and took the same to the Presidents room. It was then and there that this ever to be remembered address was written – I know many statements have been published as to where and under what circumstances the address was written – some saying in Washington, others on the train while en route to Gettysburg and some even attributing the authorship to another but based upon what the President said to us that evening of November 18th when he left us for his room and later requesting writing material I am positively sure that it was at that time and in the guest room of my sisters residence that the immortal address was composed.

Later the President and Mr. Seward were serenaded. The President made no address in response but Mr. Seward did.

The Consecration Ceremonies took place the following day, the parade to the Cemetery starting about noon, Maj. Gen. Couch being in command – the prayer of Consecration made by Rev. Dr. Stockton, the oration by Edward Everett, the dedicatory address by the President. A dirge written by James G. Percival sung and the benediction pronounced by Rev. Dr. Baugher the president of the college located at Gettysburg – The exercises were held in the southern end of the cemetery at the site now occupied by the present rostrum –

Upon completion of the ceremonies all returned to the town and the special with its distinguished officials left for Washington. As I recall the exercises, the grandeur, the immortality I may say, of the Presidents address was not at the time realized by any present except Mr. Everett. It was only a few days, however, ere the world began to realize that the words were then and there uttered that will never die.

The interments in the National Cemetery at the time of consecration number 3564 of which 979 were_____.

In conclusion allow me to quote a few lines from the oration of Gen. O. O. Howard, delivered July 4, 1865 at the laying of the Corner Stone of the Monument – "He, Abraham Lincoln, never forgot his own dedication 'till the work was finished". He did display even increased devotion of where possible. The dead did not die in vain and the Nation has experienced the new birth of freedom of which he spoke."

Very respectfully
W. G. Smyser

Assistant Quarter-Master's Office
Washington Arsenal
Capt. C. C. Able – Fort Davis, D.C.
Fort Davis Washington, DC
March 14, 1863

Governor,
I have the honor to recommend that Morrison Griffin now a
sergeant in Capt. Abells company 10th NY Artillery be
commissioned as a 2nd Lieutenant in the 10th Regiment New
York Artillery
His Excellency Horatio Seymour
Governor of New York

I am very respectfully
Your obedient servant
C C Abell
Capt. 10th N.Y. Artillery

Commanding Officer
5th N.Y. Albany
Hd Quar 5th NY Vol.
Near Hanover C. H.
June 2nd 1864

Mr. Sherman
My Dear Sir, I have to inform you that our mutual friend
Maj. A. H. White was severly if not mortally wounded in
action yesterday at Ashland on the Fredericksberg &
Richmond RR. We were required to fall back to this point
bringing off but part of our wounded some 48 in number.
The Major's wound is through the left groin passing out on
the right of the spine and he could not be moved our surgeon
remained with him and a kind lady in the village volunteered
to take him into her house and give him the best of care. His
case is a bad one yet I cannot believe but that he will live as
he seemed quite cheerful and his condition did not look bad.
At the same you wrote about his being killed he had as you
are aware he had not even been wounded. I gave your letter
to him and in writing you cannot give your full name. I think
our army will advance in a few days so as to bring Ashland
within our lines at least I hope so. Should any of his friends
or family desire to come and see him they would have to get
a pass at Washington and to Whitehouse and from thence to
the right of our army, near Hannors C. H. It is very painful to
write you such news. God grant his life may be spared. We
loose in him a dear friend and a daring brave officer.
Your Respectfully John Hammond Lt. Col.
PS
Excuse this poorly written letter it is with difficulty that I
write sitting on the ground also having been slightly
wounded yesterday which causes me some pain.
Yours JH

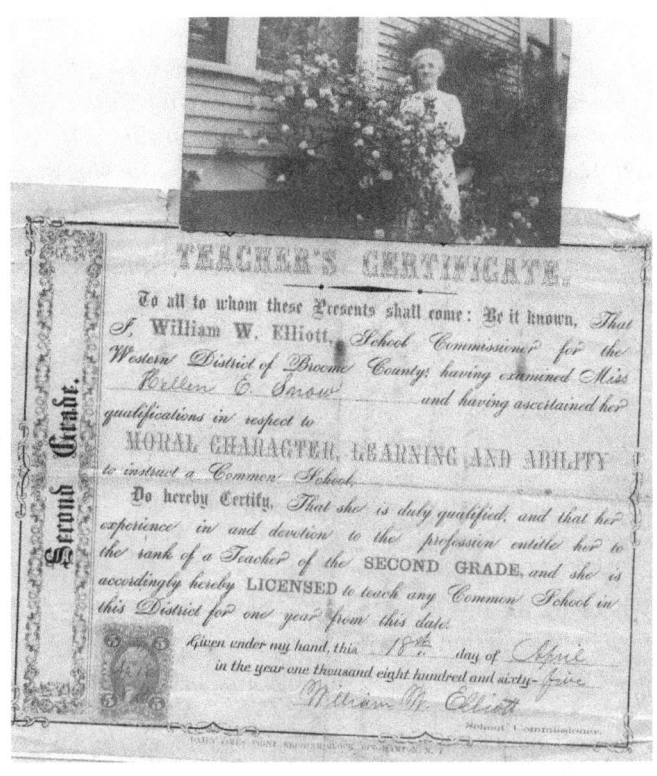

Helen earned the above school teaching certificate in 1865. – this essay about the Civil War was in a letter to her sister:
Passing Away by Helen Snow
"This beautiful day is fast drawing to a close, the bright dazzling hight of the sun will overshadow the earth. This like other days has passed away to return no more. Our once proud and happy country is now filled with war, many of its warriers have passed away, many more have gone to fill their places. If they can not restore piece there are other brave & noble hearts still left at home who will come forth and fight manfully 'till this rebellion shall have passed away. Eternity is before us but if we are mindful of our duty we shall be forever blest."

GAR

Once the War of the Rebellion ended those who served the Union joined together again...never to forget the great battles between...ourselves. **The GAR (Grand Army of the Republic)***...was the epitome of a last man club...loosing members to the "grand encampment in the sky". During the height of membership yearly conventions, or encampments, were held in locations all over the country. As time and old soldiers passed away the GAR faded into history.*

(part of a poem in a crumbling scrapbook dated 1874)
The flags are here whose bright stars shown
Through the battle's cloud with a light divine
But where are the feet that bore them on
To the very verge of the enemy's line?
And where are the lips that the bugles blew
Ah, we call the roll, but they do not come
For bugle and drum and lips are dumb
The cypress waves where the laurels grew
But Heaven's new Legion is dressed in blue.
The fairest flowers of Freedom rise
And send their fragrance to those who died-
To the **Grand Encampment in the skies.**

Pictured is an elderly GAR veteran wearing an encampment pin from 1888.

*This picture of a typical US Main Street shows the location of a **GAR Post** – on the top floor of a brick building on the left of the photo.*

Abbreviated - TIME LINE - Civil War Hostilities
From Collier's Cyclopedia – 1888
1820 – The Missouri Compromise passed. It was the settlement of the difficulty that arose regarding the question of slavery, on the proposal of admitting Missouri into the Union. Through the efforts of Henry Clay it was admitted as a slave State, under the compromise that slavery should be prohibited in all the other territories west of the Mississippi, and north of the southern boundary of Missouri.

1832 – Nullification Ordinance, passed by South Carolina threatening secession from the Union in the event of force being employed to collect the revenue at Charleston. A settlement was effected by the acceptance of Henry Clay's "compromise Bill". "States Rights" continued to be an issue of contention…

1860 – Secession of South Carolina on the election of Abraham Lincoln to the Presidency. The Southern leaders carry out threats of secession from the Union. South Carolina withdrew in December, soon followed by Mississippi, Florida, Alabama, Georgia, Louisiana and Texas. States Rights and slavery had vexed the country nearly from the formation of the Union.

1861 - Southern Confedcracy Inaugurated – on the 4th of February delegates from the seceded states met at Montgomery, Ala. and formed the Confederate Sates of America. Jefferson Davis, formerly a US Senator was chosen President.

1861 – Attack on Fort Sumter, April 12, 1861 – The Star of the West, an unarmed steamer bearing supplies to the Fort

Sumter garrison was fired upon and driven back. Southern leaders declared any attempt to relieve Fort Sumter would

be regarded as a declaration of war. Gen. Beauregard fired on the fort - after 37 hours the garrison surrendered.

1861 – March - Abraham Lincoln, 16th President of the US inaugurated

1861 – Call for 75,000 volunteers by President Lincoln to suppress the rebellion.

1861 – Seizure of Harper's Ferry by Confederate troops.

1861 – Seizure of Norfolk Navy Yard by Confederates.

1861 – Massachusetts troops attacked in the streets of Baltimore. First blood shed in the civil war is on the anniversary of Concord and Lexington – April 19.

1861 – The Confederate Congress assembled at Richmond, Virginia on July 20.

1861 – Battle of Bull Run – Federal troops drove the enemy from the field after a sharp contest - were suddenly attacked and thrown into a panic. The retreat was changed to a rout. The effect of this battle was to convince the Northern people of the desperate nature of the great conflict that had just opened. Congress immediately voted $500,000,000 and 500,000 men to prosecute the war.

1862 – Battle of the Monitor and the Merrimac March 9. This was the first battle ever fought between turreted iron ships. *(newspaper and book accounts during the war did not use the name Virginia for the ironclad, nor did time lines printed in many subsequent years)*

1862 – Invasion of Maryland by the Confederate forces under General Lee

1862 – Battle of Antietam, one of the bloodiest conflicts of the war

1862 - Battle of Fredericksburg and defeat of Union troops – loss of 12,000 federal troops.

1862 – Soux Indians on the warpath

1862 – Battle of Murfreesboro – fierce battle – losses estimated at 1/4 of number engaged – Confederate retreat

1863 - Emancipation Proclamation - freedom to slaves

1863 – Battle of Gettysburg, Penn. The backbone of the rebellion was broken - Gen. Lee was forced to retreat beyond the Potomac.

1863 – The surrender of Vicksburg with 37,000 prisoners of war in July, was one of the most important events of the war – the Confederacy was cut in two and the Mississippi opened to the Gulf.

1865 – Surrender of General Lee at Appomatox Court House, Virginia. The end of the American Civil War.

1865 – The Assassination of President Abraham Lincoln on
APRIL 14, 1865

Entered, according to Act of Congress, in the year 1865, by J. A. Arthur, in the
Clerk's Office of the District Court for the Eastern District of Pennsylvania.
WASHINGTON & LINCOLN. (APOTHEOSIS.)
B J. Ferris, Del.   Photo. and Pub. by Phil. Pho. Co., 720 Chestnut St.

Official discharge paper for Union soldier
Benjamin Cody

At the end of the great American Civil War banners were hung to celebrate the unification of the states. This picture is of the Binghamton CityHall and Fire Department. Patriotic sentiments and banners were displayed lavishly in the reunited Union.

www.ingramcontent.com/pod-product-compliance
Lightning Source LLC
Chambersburg PA
CBHW051144020726
47501CB00005B/1668